VIOLET CASTRO

ADVANCED DATA STRUCTURES FOR ALGORITHMS

Mastering Complex Data Structures for Algorithmic Problem-Solving (2024)

Copyright © 2024 by Violet Castro

All rights reserved. No part of this publication may be reproduced, stored or transmitted in any form or by any means, electronic, mechanical, photocopying, recording, scanning, or otherwise without written permission from the publisher. It is illegal to copy this book, post it to a website, or distribute it by any other means without permission.

Violet Castro asserts the moral right to be identified as the author of this work.

First edition

This book was professionally typeset on Reedsy. Find out more at reedsy.com

Contents

1 Introduction 1
2 PART 1: Advanced Lists 3
3 PART 2 : Advanced Trees 38
4 PART 3 :Disjoint Sets 97
5 PART 4 :Advanced Heapsand Priority Queues 106
6 Conclusion 167

1

Introduction

Data structures and algorithms complement each other seamlessly – algorithms rely on data structures for their functioning. This guide will walk you through more advanced data structures, enabling you to tackle even more intricate problems. It is assumed that you already possess a fundamental understanding of basic data structures and their role in algorithms.

Upon completing this guide, you should be better equipped to identify areas in your code where performance can be enhanced by implementing more sophisticated data structures. It is not expected that you grasp everything in this book on the initial read – such a feat would be nearly impossible. Instead, use this guide as a reference when evaluating whether a specific data structure suits your situation. While numerous code examples are provided, it's worth noting that this is not exclusively a programming book; various programming languages are employed to illustrate the versatility across languages.

This guide covers the following:

- A review of linked lists before delving into doubly linked lists, XOR lists, self-organizing lists, and unrolled lists.
- Advanced tree data structures like segment trees, tries, Fenwick trees, AVL trees, red-black trees, scapegoat trees, N-ary trees, and treaps.
- An exploration of disjoint sets.
- The final section is dedicated to heaps and priority queues, offering an overview of binary heaps before delving into binomial heaps, Fibonacci heaps, leftish heaps, K-ary heaps, and iterative heapsorts.

Please refrain from expecting a complete understanding on your initial pass. Take your time, progress through each section sequentially, and ensure a solid grasp of the basics before advancing to the subsequent sections.

2

PART 1: Advanced Lists

Linked Lists

Linked lists share similarities with arrays as they both belong to the category of linear data structures. However, the key distinction lies in the storage of elements in a linked list – they are not stored in contiguous locations but are instead connected using pointers.

So, what makes linked lists preferable over arrays? The rationale is straightforward. While arrays can accommodate similar types of linear data, they come with certain limitations:

1. Arrays have a fixed size, necessitating prior knowledge of the maximum number of elements they can hold. Allocated memory remains equal to the maximum number regardless of actual usage.

2. Inserting new elements in arrays is a resource-intensive

process. Creating space for new elements involves shifting existing ones. For instance, inserting a new ID, such as 1010, in a sorted array like id[] = [1000, 1020, 1040, 1060], requires moving all elements following 1000. Deletion is similarly costly due to the need to rearrange elements post-deletion.

Linked lists offer advantages over arrays:

1. They have a dynamic size.

2. Inserting and deleting elements are straightforward.

However, linked lists also come with drawbacks:

1. Random access is impractical. Elements must be accessed sequentially from the beginning, making binary search inefficient with the default linked list implementation.

2. Additional memory space is needed for each element in the form of a pointer.

3. They lack cache-friendliness as the non-contiguous nature of linked list elements eliminates reference locality present in arrays.

In the representation of linked lists, a pointer indicates the first node, also known as the head. In an empty linked list, the head possesses a NULL value. Each node in a linked list comprises data and a pointer or reference to the next node. In C language, nodes are represented using data structures, while in C# or Java, a LinkedList is represented by a class, with Nodes existing as separate classes. The LinkedList class always holds a reference of the Node class type.

This serves as an overview of linked lists, providing context for the upcoming topic.

Doubly Linked List

Doubly Linked Lists, abbreviated as DLLs, incorporate an extra pointer, commonly referred to as a previous pointer, which connects the data and the next pointer found in conventional linked lists. The structure of a DLL node in C is presented below:

```
/* Node of a doubly linked list */
  class Node
  {
  public:
  int data;
  Node* next; // Pointer to the next node in DLL
  Node* prev; // Pointer to the previous node in DLL
  };
```

Doubly linked lists offer several advantages over singly linked lists:

1. They support traversal in both forward and backward directions.
2. Deletion operations are more efficient when the pointer to the node intended for deletion is provided.
3. New nodes can be swiftly and easily inserted.

In comparison to singly linked lists, where deletion may require traversing to obtain the pointer to the preceding node, doubly linked lists utilize the previous pointer to directly access the preceding node.

However, DLLs come with a couple of drawbacks:

1. All nodes in DLLs necessitate additional space for a previous pointer.
2. Maintenance of the extra previous pointer is required for all operations. For instance, in insertion, adjustments to both the previous and next pointers are essential.

Insertions in DLLs can be executed in four ways:

At the front: Adding a new node at the front involves making the new node the new head, which is accomplished through a function named push(). This function requires a pointer to the head pointer.

```
void push(Node** head_ref, int new_data)
{
Node* new_node = new Node();
new_node->data = new_data;
new_node->next = (*head_ref);
new_node->prev = NULL;

if ((*head_ref) != NULL)
    (*head_ref)->prev = new_node;

(*head_ref) = new_node;
}
```

After a specified node: Adding a new node after a given node necessitates a function named insertAfter(), requiring a pointer to the previous node

```
void insertAfter(Node* prev_node, int new_data)
    {
    if (prev_node == NULL)
    {
    cout « "the given previous node cannot be NULL";
    return;
    }

Node* new_node = new Node();
    new_node->data = new_data;
    new_node->next = prev_node->next;
    prev_node->next = new_node;
    new_node->prev = prev_node;

if (new_node->next != NULL)
    new_node->next->prev = new_node;
    }
```

While some steps in these insertion processes mirror those for singly linked lists, additional steps are incorporated to handle the previous pointers of the head and the new node's next node in DLLs.

Adding nodes at the end.

1. Adding nodes at the end involves appending a new node to the given linked list's tail. For instance, if our DLL is 0123456789, and we append an item, 30, at the end, the DLL will become 012345678930. Since the head typically

denotes the start of the linked list, it necessitates traversing the list to the end, where the penultimate node's next pointer is modified to link to the new node.

Here are the steps to achieve this:

```
/* Given a reference (pointer to pointer) to the head
of a DLL and an int, appends a new node at the end */
void append(Node** head_ref, int new_data)
{
/* 1. Allocate a new node */
Node* new_node = new Node();
Node* last = *head_ref; /* used in step 5*/
/* 2. Set the data for the new node */
new_node->data = new_data;
/* 3. Designate this new node as the last node, making its next NULL */
new_node->next = NULL;
/* 4. If the Linked List is empty, make the new node the head */
if (*head_ref == NULL)
{
new_node->prev = NULL;
*head_ref = new_node;
return;
}
/* 5. Else traverse until the last node */
while (last->next != NULL)
last = last->next;
/* 6. Update the next of the last node */
last->next = new_node;
/* 7. Make the last node the previous node of the new node
```

```
*/
  new_node->prev = last;
  return;
}
```

Six of these steps closely resemble those used to insert a new node after a specified node in a singly linked list, with the additional step involving the adjustment of the new node's previous pointer.

Adding a node at the end

1. To add a node at the end, assuming the pointer to the given node is called next_node and the new node's data is new_data, follow these steps:
2. Verify whether next_node is NULL. If yes, the function must return since new nodes cannot be added before NULLs.
3. Allocate memory for the new node.
4. Set new_node->data = new_data.
5. The new node's previous pointer should be set as the next_node's previous node – new_node->prev = next_node->prev.
6. The next_node's previous pointer should be set as new_node – new_node->prev = new_node.
7. The new_node's next pointer should be set at next_node – new_node->next = next_node.
8. If the new_node's previous node is not NULL, set the previous node's next pointer as new_node – new_node->prev->next = new_node. If it is NULL, it becomes the head node, so (*head_ref) = new_node.

This approach is implemented through the following code block, producing the output:

```cpp
// A complete functioning C++ program demonstrating various insertion methods
#include
using namespace std;

// Definition of a linked list node
class Node
{
public:
int data;
Node* next;
Node* prev;
};

// Function to insert a new node at the front of the list
void push(Node** head_ref, int new_data)
{
// Allocate a new node
Node* new_node = new Node();

// Set the data
new_node->data = new_data;

// Make the next of the new node point to the current head and previous as NULL
new_node->next = (*head_ref);
new_node->prev = NULL;

// Change the previous of the head node to the new node
```

```cpp
    if ((*head_ref) != NULL)
    (*head_ref)->prev = new_node;

// Move the head to point to the new node
    (*head_ref) = new_node;
    }

// Function to insert a new node after a given node
    void insertAfter(Node* prev_node, int new_data)
    {
    // Check if the given prev_node is NULL
    if (prev_node == NULL)
    {
    cout << "the given previous node cannot be NULL";
    return;
    }

// Allocate a new node
    Node* new_node = new Node();

// Set the data
    new_node->data = new_data;

// Make the next of the new node point to the next of the previous node
    new_node->next = prev_node->next;

// Make the next of the previous node point to the new node
    prev_node->next = new_node;

// Make the previous of the new node point to the previous
```

node
```
    new_node->prev = prev_node;

// Change the previous of the new node's next node
    if (new_node->next != NULL)
    new_node->next->prev = new_node;
    }

// Function to append a new node at the end of the list
    void append(Node** head_ref, int new_data)
    {
    // Allocate a new node
    Node* new_node = new Node();
    Node* last = *head_ref; // used in step 5

// Set the data
    new_node->data = new_data;

// Designate this new node as the last node, making its next NULL
    new_node->next = NULL;

// If the Linked List is empty, make the new node the head
    if (*head_ref == NULL)
    {
    new_node->prev = NULL;
    *head_ref = new_node;
    return;
    }

// Else traverse until the last node
```

```cpp
    while (last->next != NULL)
    last = last->next;

// Change the next of the last node
    last->next = new_node;

// Make the last node the previous node of the new node
    new_node->prev = last;
    return;
    }

// Function to print the contents of the linked list starting from the given node
    void printList(Node* node)
    {
    Node* last;
    cout << "\nTraversal in forward direction \n";
    while (node != NULL)
    {
    cout << " " << node->data << " ";
    last = node;
    node = node->next;
    }
    cout << "\nTraversal in reverse direction \n";
    while (last != NULL)
    {
    cout << " " << last->data << " ";
    last = last->prev;
    }
    }
```

```cpp
// Driver program to test the above functions
int main()
{
    // Start with an empty list
    Node* head = NULL;

    // Insert 6. So the linked list becomes 6->NULL
    append(&head, 6);

    // Insert 7 at the beginning. So the linked list becomes 7->6->NULL
    push(&head, 7);

    // Insert 1 at the beginning. So the linked list becomes 1->7->6->NULL
    push(&head, 1);

    // Insert 4 at the end. So the linked list becomes 1->7->6->4->NULL
    append(&head, 4);

    // Insert 8, after 7. So the linked list becomes 1->7->8->6->4->NULL
    insertAfter(head->next, 8);

    cout « "Created DLL is: ";
    printList(head);
    return 0;
}
```

The expected output is:
Created DLL is:

Traversal in the forward Direction
1 7 8 6 4
Traversal in the reverse direction
4 6 8 7 1

XOR linked Lists

XOR Linked Lists offer a memory-efficient alternative to standard doubly linked lists, where each node requires two address fields for the previous and next node addresses. The XOR list employs a bitwise XOR operation in a single address field for each node, storing the XOR of addresses for the previous and next nodes.

Differences between ordinary and XOR representations are evident in how node addresses are handled:

1. **Ordinary Representation:**

   - Node A: prev = NULL, next = add(B)
   - Node B: prev = add(A), next = add(C)
   - Node C: prev = add(B), next = add(D)
   - Node D: prev = add(C), next = NULL

1. **XOR List Representation:**

   - Node A: npx = 0 XOR add(B)
   - Node B: npx = add(A) XOR add(C)
   - Node C: npx = add(B) XOR add(D)
   - Node D: npx = add(C) XOR 0

Traversal in an XOR linked list, both forward and backward, requires maintaining previously accessed node addresses to calculate the next node's address. For instance, to reach node C, node B's address is needed, achieved through an XOR of add(B) and C's npx.

Here is an implementation in C++ demonstrating this XOR-linked list:

```cpp
#include
  #include
  using namespace std;

class Node {
  public:
  int data;
  Node* xnode;
};

Node* Xor(Node* x, Node* y) {
  return reinterpret_cast(
  reinterpret_cast(x)
  ^ reinterpret_cast(y));
}

void insert(Node** head_ref, int data) {
  Node* new_node = new Node();
  new_node->data = data;
  new_node->xnode = *head_ref;

if (*head_ref != NULL) {
  (*head_ref)->xnode = Xor(new_node, (*head_ref)->xnode);
```

    }

  *head_ref = new_node;
    }

  void printList(Node* head) {
    Node* curr = head;
    Node* prev = NULL;
    Node* next;
    cout « "The nodes of the Linked List are: \n";

  while (curr != NULL) {
    cout « curr->data « " ";
    next = Xor(prev, curr->xnode);
    prev = curr;
    curr = next;
    }
    }

  int main() {
    Node* head = NULL;
    insert(&head, 10);
    insert(&head, 100);
    insert(&head, 1000);
    insert(&head, 10000);

  printList(head);
    return (0);
    }
  Output:
    10000 1000 100 10

Now that we understand how to form a doubly linked list with each node having its address field in a single space, let's delve into the implementation details. We'll focus on two key functions:

1. The first function inserts a new node at the beginning.
2. The second function traverses the list in the forward direction.

In the subsequent code example, we employ the **insert()** function to add a new node at the start. The head pointer is manipulated using a double-pointer. Consider the following points:

- The XOR of the next and previous nodes is stored in each node as **npx**.
- **npx** is the sole address member within each node.
- When a new node is inserted at the beginning, the **npx** of the new node is always the XOR of NULL and the current head.
- The **npx** of the current head must be updated to the XOR of the new node and the node beside the current head.

For forward traversal, the **printList** function is utilized to print the data values in each node. Obtaining the address of the next node involves tracking the current and previous nodes. An XOR of **curr->npx** and **prev** provides the address of the next node.

Here's an example of the code:
#include
#include

```cpp
using namespace std;

class Node {
  public:
    int data;
    Node* npx; /* The XOR of the next and previous node */
};

Node* XOR(Node* a, Node* b) {
    return reinterpret_cast(
    reinterpret_cast(a) ^
    reinterpret_cast(b));
}

void insert(Node** head_ref, int data) {
    Node* new_node = new Node();
    new_node->data = data;
    new_node->npx = *head_ref;

if (*head_ref != NULL) {
    (*head_ref)->npx = XOR(new_node, (*head_ref)->npx);
    }

*head_ref = new_node;
    }

void printList(Node* head) {
    Node* curr = head;
    Node* prev = NULL;
    Node* next;
    cout << "Following are the nodes of Linked List: \n";
```

```
while (curr != NULL) {
    cout << curr->data << " ";
    next = XOR(prev, curr->npx);
    prev = curr;
    curr = next;
    }
}

int main() {
    Node* head = NULL;
    insert(&head, 10);
    insert(&head, 20);
    insert(&head, 30);
    insert(&head, 40);

printList(head);
    return (0);
    }
```

Output:
Following are the nodes of Linked List:
40 30 20 10

Note: The XOR of pointers is not defined by C and C++ standards on every platform, so this implementation may not work universally.

Organizing themselves based on a heuristic to enhance access times, self-organizing lists strategically reorder their elements. The primary objective is to optimize linear search efficiency by prioritizing frequently accessed items towards the front of the list. This reordering aims for near-constant time in the best-case scenario for element access.

Two search scenarios exist: online, where the search sequence is unknown, and offline, where the entire search sequence is known in advance. In offline searches, nodes may be arranged based on decreasing search frequencies, with the most frequently searched element positioned first and the least searched placed last. However, real-world applications often lack upfront knowledge of the search sequence.

Self-organizing lists dynamically reorder themselves after each search, aiming to leverage locality of reference. In many databases, 20% of items cover 80% of searches.

Now, let's explore three strategies employed by self-organizing lists:

1. **Move-To-Front Method:** This method brings the most recently searched item to the list's front, simplifying implementation. However, it tends to prioritize even infrequently searched items, potentially impacting access time negatively.

Here is an example:

```
// CPP Program to implement self-organizing list
// using the move-to-front method
#include
using namespace std;

struct self_list {
  int value;
  struct self_list* next;
};

self_list* head = NULL, *rear = NULL;
```

```
void insert_self_list(int number) {
  self_list* temp = new self_list();
  temp->value = number;
  temp->next = NULL;

if (head == NULL)
  head = rear = temp;
  else {
  rear->next = temp;
  rear = temp;
  }
  }

bool search_self_list(int key) {
  self_list* current = head;
  self_list* prev = NULL;

while (current != NULL) {
  if (current->value == key) {
  if (prev != NULL) {
  prev->next = current->next;
  current->next = head;
  head = current;
  }
  return true;
  }
  prev = current;
  current = current->next;
  }
  return false;
  }
```

```cpp
void display() {
    if (head == NULL) {
        cout << "List is empty" << endl;
        return;
    }

    self_list* temp = head;
    cout << "List: ";
    while (temp != NULL) {
        cout << temp->value;
        if (temp->next != NULL)
        cout << " —> ";
        temp = temp->next;
    }
    cout << endl << endl;
}

int main() {
    insert_self_list(1);
    insert_self_list(2);
    insert_self_list(3);
    insert_self_list(4);
    insert_self_list(5);

    display();

    if (search_self_list(4))
        cout << "Searched: 4" << endl;
    else
        cout << "Not Found: 4" << endl;
```

```
display();

if (search_self_list(2))
   cout « "Searched: 2" « endl;
else
   cout « "Not Found: 2" « endl;

display();

return 0;
}
```
Output:
List: 1 —> 2 —> 3 —> 4 —> 5
Searched: 4
List: 4 —> 1 —> 2 —> 3 —> 5
Searched: 2
List: 2 —> 4 —> 1 —> 3 —> 5

2. The Count Method

The count method involves maintaining a record of how frequently a node is searched, essentially tracking its search frequency. Each node possesses additional storage, with this count incrementing upon each search. Subsequently, nodes are organized in a manner where the most frequently searched node is positioned at the front of the list.

Consider the following examples:

- **Example 1:**
- Input: List: 1, 2, 3, 4, 5 Searched: 4
- Output: List: 4, 1, 2, 3, 5
- **Example 2:**
- Input: List: 4, 1, 2, 3, 5 Searched: 5 Searched: 5 Searched:

2
- Output: List: 5, 2, 4, 1, 3

In this method, nodes are arranged based on their search frequencies. For instance, if a node, like 5 in the second example, is searched twice, it is moved to the head of the list. When multiple nodes have similar frequencies, their order is maintained based on their insertion sequence.

The provided C++ program demonstrates the implementation of a self-organizing list using the count method. Nodes are inserted, searched, and the list is displayed, showcasing the rearrangements based on search frequencies.

```
// C++ Program to implement self-organizing list
// using the count method
#include
using namespace std;

struct self_list {
    int value;
    int count;
    struct self_list* next;
};

self_list *head = NULL, *rear = NULL;

// Function to insert an element into the list
    void insert_self_list(int number) {
    self_list* temp = new self_list();
    temp->value = number;
    temp->count = 0;
    temp->next = NULL;
```

```
if (head == NULL)
  head = rear = temp;
  else {
  rear->next = temp;
  rear = temp;
  }
}

// Function to search the key in the list
  // and rearrange the self-organizing list
  bool search_self_list(int key) {
  self_list* current = head;
  self_list* prev = NULL;

while (current != NULL) {
  if (current->value == key) {
  current->count = current->count + 1;

if (current != head) {
  self_list* temp = head;
  self_list* temp_prev = NULL;

while (current->count < temp->count) {
  temp_prev = temp;
  temp = temp->next;
  }

if (current != temp) {
  prev->next = current->next;
  current->next = temp;
```

```cpp
        if (temp == head)
            head = current;
        else
            temp_prev->next = current;
        }
    }
    return true;
    }
    prev = current;
    current = current->next;
    }
    return false;
    }


// Function to display the list
    void display() {
    if (head == NULL) {
    cout << "List is empty" << endl;
    return;
    }

self_list* temp = head;
    cout << "List: ";
    while (temp != NULL) {
    cout << temp->value << "(" << temp->count << ")";
    if (temp->next != NULL)
    cout << " —> ";
    temp = temp->next;
    }
    cout << endl << endl;
    }
```

```
// Driver Code
  int main() {
  insert_self_list(1);
  insert_self_list(2);
  insert_self_list(3);
  insert_self_list(4);
  insert_self_list(5);

display();

search_self_list(4);
  search_self_list(2);
  display();

search_self_list(4);
  search_self_list(4);
  search_self_list(5);
  display();

search_self_list(5);
  search_self_list(2);
  search_self_list(2);
  search_self_list(2);
  display();

return 0;
  }
```
  Output:
  List: 1(0) —> 2(0) —> 3(0) —> 4(0) —> 5(0)
  List: 2(1) —> 4(1) —> 1(0) —> 3(0) —> 5(0)
  List: 4(3) —> 5(1) —> 2(1) —> 1(0) —> 3(0)

List: 2(4) —> 4(3) —> 5(2) —> 1(0) —> 3(0)

3. The Transpose Method

The transpose method involves swapping the accessed node with its predecessor. Essentially, when a node is accessed, it exchanges places with the one preceding it. The exception to this rule is when the accessed node is already at the head. In simpler terms, the priority of an accessed node gradually increases until it reaches the head position. Notably, this method requires multiple accesses to move a node to the head.

Consider the following examples:

- **Example 1:**
- Input: List: 1, 2, 3, 4, 5, 6 Searched: 4
- Output: List: 1, 2, 4, 3, 5, 6
- **Example 2:**
- Input: List: 1, 2, 4, 3, 5, 6 Searched: 5
- Output: List: 1, 2, 4, 5, 3, 6

Explanation:

- In the first case, node 4 is swapped with node 3, its predecessor.
- In the second case, node 5 is swapped with its predecessor, which is node 3.

The provided C++ program illustrates the implementation of a self-organizing list using the transpose method. Nodes are inserted, searched, and the list is displayed, showcasing the rearrangements based on the transpose strategy.

// C++ Program to implement self-organizing list

```cpp
// using the transpose method
#include
using namespace std;

struct self_list {
   int value;
   struct self_list* next;
};

self_list *head = NULL, *rear = NULL;

// Function to insert an element into the list
   void insert_self_list(int number) {
   self_list* temp = new self_list();
   temp->value = number;
   temp->next = NULL;

if (head == NULL)
   head = rear = temp;
   else {
   rear->next = temp;
   rear = temp;
   }
}

// Function to search the key in the list
   // and rearrange the self-organizing list
   bool search_self_list(int key) {
   self_list* current = head;
   self_list* prev = NULL;
   self_list* prev_prev = NULL;
```

```
while (current != NULL) {
  if (current->value == key) {
  if (prev_prev != NULL) {
  prev_prev->next = current;
  prev->next = current->next;
  current->next = prev;
  } else if (prev != NULL) {
  prev->next = current->next;
  current->next = prev;
  head = current;
  }
  return true;
  }
  prev_prev = prev;
  prev = current;
  current = current->next;
  }
  return false;
  }

// Function to display the list
  void display() {
  if (head == NULL) {
  cout « "List is empty" « endl;
  return;
  }

self_list* temp = head;
  cout « "List: ";
  while (temp != NULL) {
  cout « temp->value;
```

```cpp
        if (temp->next != NULL)
        cout << " —> ";
        temp = temp->next;
    }
    cout << endl << endl;
}

// Driver Code
int main() {
    insert_self_list(1);
    insert_self_list(2);
    insert_self_list(3);
    insert_self_list(4);
    insert_self_list(5);
    insert_self_list(6);

display();

search_self_list(4);
    display();

search_self_list(5);
    display();

return 0;
}
```

Output:
List: 1 —> 2 —> 3 —> 4 —> 5 —> 6
Searched: 4
List: 1 —> 2 —> 4 —> 3 —> 5 —> 6
Searched: 5

List: 1 —> 2 —> 4 —> 5 —> 3 —> 6

Unrolled Linked List

Unrolled linked lists represent a variation of linked list data structures. In contrast to traditional linked lists storing a single element per node, unrolled linked lists store entire arrays at each node. This innovative approach combines the advantages of arrays, offering minimal memory overhead, with the efficiency of linked lists in terms of swift insertion and deletion. The amalgamation of these benefits results in significantly enhanced overall performance.

The distinctive feature of unrolled linked lists lies in their ability to distribute overheads, typically pointers, by accommodating multiple elements within each node. For instance, if a node holds an array with four elements, the associated overhead is distributed across those elements.

Unrolled linked lists demonstrate superior performance, particularly considering the cache management capabilities of modern CPUs. Although the per-node overhead is relatively high when compared to standard linked lists, this drawback becomes insignificant in the context of the benefits it provides in contemporary computing environments.

Properties

Unrolled linked lists essentially function as linked lists where nodes store an array of values rather than a single value. The array within each node can encompass various data types, similar to standard arrays, including abstract data types and primitive types. Nodes have a predetermined maximum capacity, and the average implementation ensures an average capacity of 3/4. This is achieved by redistributing values between arrays as needed.

While unrolled linked lists entail a slightly higher per-node overhead due to storing the maximum number of values per array, the per-value overhead is lower than that of standard linked lists. As the maximum size of each array increases, the average space required for each value decreases. This is particularly advantageous for small data types, such as bits, offering additional space efficiency.

In essence, an unrolled linked list seamlessly combines the advantages of a standard linked list and an array. It leverages the rapid indexing and storage locality benefits of an array, coupled with the node insertion and deletion advantages from a linked list.

Insertion and Deletion

The algorithm for inserting or deleting elements in unrolled linked lists varies based on the implementation. Typically, a low-water mark of around 50% is maintained. When inserting an element exceeds the node's capacity, a new node is created, and 50% of the elements from the original array are transferred. Conversely, if an element removal results in less than 50% occupancy, elements from the adjacent array are moved to maintain 50%. If this leads to both nodes falling below 50%, they are merged.

On average, nodes in unrolled linked lists achieve a utilization of 70-75%, resulting in minimal overhead compared to standard linked lists. The low-water mark can be adjusted to optimize list performance, with increased utilization requiring more frequent splitting and merging operations.

Algorithm Pseudocode

The insertion and deletion algorithm is outlined as follows. Nodes contain an array named 'data,' the number of elements in the array 'numElements,' and a 'next' pointer to the subsequent node.

Insert(newElement)

Find node in linked list e
   If e.numElements < e.data.size
   e.data.push(newElement)
   e.numElements ++
   Else
   Create new Node e1
   Move the final half of e.data into e1.data
   e.numElements = e.numElements / 2
   e1.data.push(newElement)
   e1.numElements = e1.data.size / 2 + 1

Delete(element)

Find element in node e
   e.data.remove(element)
   e.numElements —
   While e.numElements < e.data.size / 2
   Put element from e.next.data in e.data
   e.next.numElements —
   e.numElements ++
   If e.next.numElements < e.next.data.size / 2
   Merge nodes e and e.next
   Delete node e.next

Programmers have flexibility in implementing these functions. For instance, in the Insert function, the choice of which node to insert into can be determined based on specific criteria such as grouping or sorting, depending on the nature of the data being handled.

Time and Space Complexity of Unrolled Linked Lists

Analyzing an unrolled linked list poses challenges due to diverse implementation methods and data-dependent variations. However, the amortization across array elements contributes to favorable time and space analyses.

Time Complexity: Inserting an element involves locating the target node, incurring a time complexity of $O(n)$. If the node isn't full, the operation concludes. Creating a new node, required when the node is full, is a constant-time process, independent of the total linked list values. Deletion operates similarly in reverse, leveraging constant-time operations and swift pointer updates between linked nodes, irrespective of list size. Indexing, crucial in unrolled linked lists, relies on caching.

Operation Complexity:

- Insertion: $O(n)$
- Deletion: $O(n)$
- Indexing: $O(n)$
- Search: $O(n)$

It's crucial to emphasize that the practical benefits of unrolled linked lists emerge in real-world applications, not just in asymptotic analyses.

Space Complexity: The space required by an unrolled linked list ranges from $(v/m)n$ to $2(v/m)n^2$, where 'v' indicates each node's overhead, 'm' indicates the maximum number of elements per node, and 'n' indicates the number of nodes.

Despite resembling the asymptotic space of other linear data structures, unrolled linked lists exhibit superior space efficiency as overheads are distributed across multiple elements.

Caching: The true advantages of unrolled linked lists lie in caching, particularly for indexing. In memory access, fetching the entire page occurs, leading to a cache miss if the desired value is not found. Unrolled linked lists experience a maximum of $m/n + 1$ cache misses during indexing, outperforming standard linked lists by a factor of 'm'. Further analysis, considering cache line size 'B,' often aligns with the optimal fetching value of $(m/B)(m/B)$. Traversing each node involves (n/B) cache misses, and the entire list can be traversed in $(m/n + 1)(n/B)$, closely approaching the optimal cache miss value of $(m/B)(m/B)$.

In Part 2, we will delve into advanced tree structures.

3

PART 2 : Advanced Trees

Segment Trees

Segment trees become essential when numerous range queries on arrays are required, coupled with simultaneous array element modifications. For instance, tasks may involve determining the sum of array elements from indices L to R or finding the minimum within the Range Minimum Query Problem. This data structure, the segment tree, proves remarkably versatile in addressing such challenges and more.

In essence, a segment tree is a binary tree storing intervals, with each node representing one such interval. Consider an array A of size N and a corresponding segment tree T:

- The root of T represents the entire array A[0:N-1].
- Each leaf in T signifies an element A[i], satisfying $0 \leq i < N$.
- Internal nodes of T represent unions of elementary intervals A[i:j], where $0 \leq i < j < N$.

The root initially represents the entire array, further divided into two half intervals, represented by the root's children: $A[0:(N-1)/2]$ and $A[(N-1)/2+1:(N-1)]$. Through successive steps, each segment gets divided, with the two children embodying the halves. The tree's height is $log2N$, N leaves aligning with array elements, and N-1 internal nodes in total, resulting in 2xN-1 nodes.

Once constructed, the structure of a segment tree remains fixed, yet node values can be updated. The segment tree supports two operations:

1. **Update:** Modifies an array A element and updates the tree accordingly.
2. **Query:** Interrogates segments or intervals, delivering specific problem answers like summation, minimum, or maximum in the designated segment.

Implementing a Segment Tree:

Represented as a binary tree, the segment tree can be expressed linearly. Prior to building it, determining the node's content is essential. For instance, if the goal is to find the sum of array elements from indices L to R, each node stores the sum of its children nodes, except for leaf nodes.

Recursion facilitates a bottom-up approach to build the segment tree, starting from leaves and progressing to the root. Leaf nodes represent individual elements, and each recursive step forms internal parental nodes, signifying unions between children's intervals. The merging process varies based on the query, with recursion concluding at the root, representing the entire array.

Updating: Updating involves locating the leaf with the element to be modified. This is achieved by traversing either the left or right child, depending on the relevant interval. Once found, the leaf undergoes updating, with changes cascading from the leaf to the root through a bottom-up approach.

Querying: To query a tree for a range from L to R, commence at the root and recurse, verifying if the node's represented interval entirely fits within that range. If so, the node's value is returned. Queries and updates can be executed in any sequence.

How to Use a Segment Tree: Determining the stored content in a tree node precedes its construction. For summation purposes within the l to r interval, each node must sum the elements in its represented interval. The build process involves recursion, starting at the root and progressing to the leaves. Returning from leaves to the root, all nodes along the path undergo updating. The current node to be processed is denoted by .node, with left and right nodes represented by 2xnode and 2xnode+1, respectively. The interval a node represents is defined by start and end, with the build complexity being O(N).

For element updates, identification of the interval containing the element is required, followed by recursion on the left or right child. The update complexity is O(logN).

When querying a specific range, three conditions are checked:

1. The node's represented range is entirely outside the specified range (returns 0).
2. The node's represented range is entirely inside the speci-

fied range (returns the node's sum).
3. The node's represented range is partly in and partly outside the specified range (returns the sum of left and right children). The query complexity is O(logN).

In summary, segment trees prove invaluable for efficient range queries and array modifications, providing an effective solution to a multitude of problems.

Trie Data Structures

The term "Trie" originates from "retrieval," and it represents a structured tree data system designed for storing collections of strings. In this arrangement, the count of pointers corresponds to the number of alphabet characters present in each node, allowing for efficient word retrieval based on prefixes. For instance, if strings are constructed using the alphabet letters a to z, each trie node may have a maximum of 26 pointers.

Also known as a prefix or digital tree, a trie's hierarchical placement determines its associated key. Key properties for a set of strings include:

1. The root node invariably signifies the null node.
2. The children of each node are sorted alphabetically.
3. Each node may have up to 26 children, representing letters from a to z.
4. Except for the root, each node can store a single alphabet letter.

Basic Operations

Trie operations revolve around three fundamental actions:

1. **Inserting a Node:**

- Each letter of the word (input key) is individually inserted into the Trie_node, with children pointing to subsequent Trie node levels.
- The key array of characters serves as an index for children.
- If a reference to the current letter exists in the present node, the node should be set to the referenced node. Otherwise, a new node is created, the letter is set equal to the current one, and the present node starts with the new node.
- The length of the character determines the trie's depth.

Implementation of node insertion involves a class named **Data_Trie**, with a method for inserting words.

1. **Searching a Node:**

- Searching a node mirrors the process of inserting a node, focusing on key search.
- The search operation is encapsulated within a class named **Search_Trie**.

1. **Deleting a Node:**

- Deletion is contingent upon the successful identification of the specified key; otherwise, the operation ceases.
- If the key is found, it is deleted.

Implementation of the deletion process is managed through the **Node_delete** method within the class structure, considering various conditions and ensuring the integrity of the trie structure.

In summary, Trie data structures offer an organized and efficient means of managing sets of strings, with well-defined operations for insertion, search, and deletion.

Applications of Trie Data Structures

Trie data structures find utility in several applications, offering unique advantages and some limitations. Here are a few notable applications:

1. **Spell Checker:** Tries play a crucial role in spellchecking processes, encompassing three essential steps. Firstly, they efficiently locate the required word in the dictionary. Subsequently, the trie facilitates the generation of relevant suggestions. Finally, these suggestions are sorted, ensuring the desired word prominently appears at the top. Tries store dictionary words, enhancing the spell checker's ability to swiftly identify words in the underlying data structure. This not only simplifies word retrieval but also facilitates the development of algorithms incorporating pertinent word collections.
2. **Auto-Complete:** Widely employed in mobile apps, internet interfaces, and text editors, auto-complete functionality streamlines the process of finding alternative word suggestions. Key features include an alphabetical filtering of entries based on the node's key and the ability to trace pointers to the node representing the user-entered string. As users begin typing, auto-complete actively predicts and attempts to finish the input, enhancing user experience and efficiency.

3. **Browser History:** Tries are instrumental in completing URLs in web browsers. Leveraging the trie structure, browsers maintain a record of visited websites in an organized manner, enabling users to easily retrieve desired URLs from their browsing history.

Advantages:

- Simplifies the insertion process, offering faster string search capabilities compared to standard binary trees and hash tables.
- Provides an entry filter in alphabetical order based on the node's key, enhancing efficiency.

Disadvantages:

- Requires more memory for string storage.
- Falls short in speed when compared to hash tables.

In essence, Trie data structures prove invaluable in diverse applications, optimizing processes such as spell checking, auto-complete features, and browser history management. While exhibiting notable advantages, it's essential to consider the associated limitations, particularly in terms of memory usage and speed compared to alternative data structures.

Fenwick Tree Overview

Fenwick trees, also known as binary indexed trees (BIT), provide an efficient means of representing arrays of numbers and calculating prefix sums. Consider an array [2, 3, -1, 0, 6]. The prefix sum, derived from the first three elements [2, 3, -1], is calculated as 2 + 3 + -1 = 4. Efficient prefix sum calculation is crucial in various scenarios, motivating a closer look.

Imagine having an array a[] and needing two distinct operations:

1. **Point Update Operation:** Modify the value stored at index i.
2. **Range Sum Query:** Obtain the sum of a prefix of length k.

Here is a simple implementation of these operations:
```
int a[] = {2, 1, 4, 6, -1, 5, -32, 0, 1};

void update(int i, int v) {
   a[i] = v;
}

int prefixSum(int k) {
   int sum = 0;
   for (int i = 0; i < k; i++)
   sum += a[i];
   return sum;
}
```
While this solution is effective, the drawback lies in the time needed for prefix sum calculation, proportional to the array

length. This becomes a limitation when dealing with large numbers and intermingled operations. While a segment tree offers an efficient solution with O(logN) time complexity for both operations, the Fenwick tree, or BIT tree, presents an alternative.

Despite the Fenwick tree's ability to perform both operations in O(logN) time, its simplicity and space efficiency make it a practical choice over a segment tree. BIT trees require minimal code, typically no more than 10 lines.

Before delving into the BIT tree, let's explore a bit manipulation trick: how to isolate the last bit set in a binary number. The expression x & (-x) achieves this by leveraging the 2's complement of x.

Understanding this bit manipulation trick becomes essential as we proceed into a deeper exploration of the BIT tree.

Binary Indexed Tree Concept

Understanding the concept of a Binary Indexed Tree (BIT) involves recognizing its parallel to the representation of integers using powers of two. Similarly, for an array of size N, a BIT array, denoted as BIT[], can be maintained to store the sum of specific numbers from the array at any given index. This structure is commonly referred to as a partial sum tree.

To illustrate how partial sums are stored in BIT[], consider the following example:

```
// Ensure our given array is 1-based indexed
   int a[] = {0, 1, 2, 3, 4, 5, 6, 7, 8, 9, 10, 11, 12, 13, 14, 15, 16};
```

In the accompanying image of the BIT tree, enclosed boxes represent the value

BIT[index], with partial sums stored in each BIT[index]. Note the pattern:

- If x is odd, BIT[x] is equal to a[x].
- If x is a power of 2, BIT[x] equals the sum of a[1] through a[x].

Cumulative sums from index i to i-(1«r)+1 (both inclusive) are stored in each index i in the BIT[] array, with r representing the last set bit in index i. For instance:

- Sum of the first 12 numbers in array a[]: BIT[12] + BIT[8] = (a[12]+...+a[9]) + (a[8]+...+a[1])
- Similarly, the sum of the first 6 elements: BIT[6] + BIT[4] = (a[6]+a[5]) + (a[4]+...+a[1])
- Sum of the first 8 elements: BIT[8] = a[8]+...+a[1]

Constructing the BIT tree involves initializing a BIT[] array with values set to 0 and subsequently calling the update() operation for each element in the given array, thus constructing the Binary Indexed Tree. The update() operation, adding "val" at index "x," is performed through a for loop that runs in O(logN) time.

The query operation, returning the sum of the first x elements in array a[], is implemented as follows:

```
int query(int x) {
int sum = 0;
for(; x > 0; x -= x&-x)
sum += BIT[x];
return sum;
}
```

This query operation also operates in O(logN) time, where the loop iterates over the number of bits in x, which is N at most. The complete program incorporates these principles into a practical implementation, showcasing the efficiency of the Binary Indexed Tree in managing prefix sums.

Determining When to Use BIT or Fenwick Trees

Before opting for the utilization of BIT (Binary Indexed Tree) or Fenwick Trees for range-based operations, it is crucial to assess whether the function or operation at hand satisfies certain criteria:

1. **Associativity:** Ensure that the operation is associative, meaning $((,),)=(,(,))f(f(a,b),c)=f(a,f(b,c))$. This criterion applies to both BIT and segment trees.
2. **Inverse Existence:** Check if the operation has an inverse. For instance, addition has an inverse in subtraction, multiplication has an inverse in division, and so forth. GCD (greatest common divisor) lacks an inverse, making BIT unsuitable for calculating range GCDs.
3. **Space Complexity:** Consider the space complexity, which is $()O(N)$ to declare another array of size N.
4. **Time Complexity:** Assess the time complexity, which is $(\log□)O(\log N)$ for each operation, including queries and updates.

Applications of BIT

BIT finds primary applications in two domains:

1. **Arithmetic Coding Algorithm:** BIT is employed in im-

plementing the arithmetic coding algorithm, showcasing its utility in specific operations.
2. **Counting Inversions in Arrays:** BIT is used for efficiently counting inversions in arrays, achieving a time complexity of $O(N \log N)$.

AVL Tree Overview

The AVL tree, conceived in 1962 by GM Adelson-Velsky and EM Landis, is a height-balanced binary search tree. Each node in the AVL tree possesses a balance factor, determined by subtracting the right subtree's height from the left subtree's height. The balance factor, denoted as k, should ideally range between -1 and +1 for each node, indicating a balanced tree.

- If $k=1$, the left subtree is one level higher than the right subtree.
- If $k=0$, the left and right subtrees are of equal height.
- If $k=-1$, the left subtree is one level lower than the right subtree.

Complexity of AVL Tree Operations

The complexity of AVL tree operations is summarized as follows:

Algorithm	Average Case	Worst Case
Space	O(N)	O(N)
Search	O(log N)	O(log N)
Insert	O(log N)	O(log N)
Delete	O(log N)	O(log N)

AVL Tree Operations

As a binary search tree, AVL tree operations are consistent with standard binary search tree operations. Searching or traversing an AVL tree adheres to the properties, while insertions and deletions may disturb the tree's balance. In such cases, rotations are employed to restore balance, a process to be discussed shortly.

Advantages of Utilizing AVL Trees

AVL trees offer precise control over the height of binary search trees, preventing them from becoming skewed or unbalanced. In traditional binary search trees, operations take $()O(h)$ time, where h is the height. However, if the tree becomes skewed, the time complexity can escalate to $()O(N)$. By limiting the height to log☐log$N$, AVL trees establish an upper bound on every operation, ensuring it remains within (log☐)$O(\log N)$, where N signifies the number of nodes.

Rotations in AVL Trees

Rotations are employed in AVL trees only when the balance factor deviates from -1, 0, or +1. Four types of rotations exist:

1. **LL Rotation:** Triggered when the inserted node is in the left subtree of A's left subtree.
2. **RR Rotation:** Applied when the inserted node is in the right subtree of A's right subtree.
3. **LR Rotation:** A double rotation, combining RR and LL rotations, performed on the subtree where the inserted node deviates from the balanced range.
4. **RL Rotation:** Similar to LR rotation but involves LL and RR rotations.

In these cases, A denotes the node with a balance factor outside the -1 to +1 range. LL and RR rotations are single rotations, while LR and RL rotations are double rotations. A tree must have a minimum height of 2 to be considered unbalanced.

Illustration of Rotation Types:

1. **RR Rotation:**

- Unbalanced due to insertion into the right subtree of A's right subtree.
- An anticlockwise RR rotation is applied.

1. **LL Rotation:**

- Imbalance arises from insertion into the left subtree of C's left subtree.
- A clockwise LL rotation is executed.

1. **LR Rotation:**

- A combination of RR and LL rotations.
- RR rotation on the subtree and LL rotation on the full tree.

1. **RL Rotation:**

- Combines LL and RR rotations.
- LL rotation on the subtree and RR rotation on the full tree.

Implementation of AVL Tree in C++

Below is a C++ program demonstrating AVL tree operations, including insertion and deletion:

#include

```cpp
using namespace std;

class AVLNode {
    public:
    int key;
    AVLNode *left;
    AVLNode *right;
    int depth;
};

// Function to get the maximum of two integers
    int max(int a, int b) {
    return (a > b) ? a : b;
    }

// Function to get the height of the tree
    int depth(AVLNode *n) {
    if (n == NULL)
    return 0;
    return n->depth;
    }

// Function to allocate a new node with a given key
    AVLNode* newNode(int key) {
    AVLNode* node = new AVLNode();
    node->key = key;
    node->left = NULL;
    node->right = NULL;
    node->depth = 1; // New node added as a leaf
    return(node);
    }
```

```
// Right rotate the subtree rooted with y
  AVLNode *rightRotate(AVLNode *y) {
  AVLNode *x = y->left;
  AVLNode *T2 = x->right;

// Perform rotation
  x->right = y;
  y->left = T2;

// Update heights
  y->depth = max(depth(y->left), depth(y->right)) + 1;
  x->depth = max(depth(x->left), depth(x->right)) + 1;

// Return new root
  return x;
  }


// Left rotate the subtree rooted with x
  AVLNode *leftRotate(AVLNode *x) {
  AVLNode *y = x->right;
  AVLNode *T2 = y->left;

// Perform rotation
  y->left = x;
  x->right = T2;

// Update heights
  x->depth = max(depth(x->left), depth(x->right)) + 1;
  y->depth = max(depth(y->left), depth(y->right)) + 1;

// Return new root
```

```
    return y;
}

// Get balance factor of node N
    int getBalance(AVLNode *N) {
    if (N == NULL)
    return 0;
    return depth(N->left) - depth(N->right);
}

// Insertion operation for a node in AVL tree
    AVLNode* insert(AVLNode* node, int key) {
    // Normal BST insertion
    if (node == NULL)
    return(newNode(key));
    if (key < node->key)
    node->left = insert(node->left, key);
    else if (key > node->key)
    node->right = insert(node->right, key);
    else // Equal keys not allowed
    return node;

// Update height of the ancestor node
    node->depth = 1 + max(depth(node->left), depth(node->right));

int balance = getBalance(node); // Get balance factor

// Rotate if unbalanced
    // Left Left Case
    if (balance > 1 && key < node->left->key)
```

```
    return rightRotate(node);

// Right Right Case
   if (balance < -1 && key > node->right->key)
   return leftRotate(node);

// Left Right Case
   if (balance > 1 && key > node->left->key) {
   node->left = leftRotate(node->left);
   return rightRotate(node);
   }

// Right Left Case
   if (balance < -1 && key < node->right->key) {
   node->right = rightRotate(node->right);
   return leftRotate(node);
   }

return node;
   }

// Find the node with the minimum value
   AVLNode * minValueNode(AVLNode* node) {
   AVLNode* current = node;

// Find the leftmost leaf
   while (current->left != NULL)
   current = current->left;

return current;
   }
```

```c
// Delete a node from AVL tree with the given key
AVLNode* deleteNode(AVLNode* root, int key) {
    if (root == NULL)
        return root;

    // Perform BST delete
    if ( key < root->key )
        root->left = deleteNode(root->left, key);
    else if( key > root->key )
        root->right = deleteNode(root->right, key);
    else {
        // Node with only one child or no child
        if( (root->left == NULL) || (root->right == NULL) ) {
            AVLNode *temp = root->left ? root->left : root->right;
            if (temp == NULL) {
                temp = root;
                root = NULL;
            } else // One child case
                *root = *temp;
            free(temp);
        }
        else {
            // Node with two children
            AVLNode* temp = minValueNode(root->right);

            // Copy the inorder successor's data to this node
            root->key = temp->key;

            // Delete the inorder successor
            root->right = deleteNode(root->right, temp->key);
        }
```

```
    }

  if (root == NULL)
    return root;

  // Update depth
    root->depth = 1 + max(depth(root->left), depth(root->right));

  // Get balance factor
    int balance = getBalance(root);

  // Rotate the tree if unbalanced
    // Left Left Case
    if (balance > 1 && getBalance(root->left) >= 0)
    return rightRotate(root);

  // Left Right Case
    if (balance > 1 && getBalance(root->left) < 0) {
    root->left = leftRotate(root->left);
    return rightRotate(root);
    }

  // Right Right Case
    if (balance < -1 && getBalance(root->right) <= 0)
    return leftRotate(root);

  // Right Left Case
    if (balance < -1 && getBalance(root->right) > 0) {
    root->right = rightRotate(root->right);
    return leftRotate(root);
    }
```

```cpp
    return root;
  }

// In-order traversal of the AVL tree
  void inOrder(AVLNode *root) {
  if(root != NULL) {
  inOrder(root->left);
  cout << root->key << " ";
  inOrder(root->right);
  }
  }

// Main code
  int main() {
  AVLNode *root = NULL;

// Constructing an AVL tree
  root = insert(root, 12);
  root = insert(root, 8);
  root = insert(root, 18);
  root = insert(root, 5);
  root = insert(root, 11);
  root = insert(root, 17);
  root = insert(root, 4);

// In-order traversal for the above tree: 4 5 8 11 12 17 18
  cout << "In-order traversal for the AVL tree is: \n";
  inOrder(root);

root = deleteNode(root, 5);
  cout << "\nIn-order traversal after deletion of node 5: \n";
```

```
inOrder(root);

return 0;
}
```
Output:
In-order traversal for the AVL tree is:
4 5 8 11 12 17 18
In-order traversal after deletion of node 5:
4 8 11 12 17 18

Red-Black Trees: A Balanced Binary Tree Variant

Red-black trees, a variation of self-balancing binary trees conceptualized by Rudolf Bayer in 1972, introduce an additional attribute—color (either red or black)—to each node. This innovative approach maintains balance by examining node colors along the path from the root to a leaf, ensuring no path exceeds twice the length of any other, thus preserving equilibrium.

Properties of Red-Black Trees:

1. The root must consistently be black.
2. NILs are universally acknowledged as black, implying that all non-NIL nodes possess two children.
3. Children of red nodes are invariably black.
4. The black height rule establishes, for a specific node v, an integer $()bh(v)$ such that a designated path leading to a NIL from v comprises the correct $()bh(v)$ real nodes. The black height of the red-black tree is defined by the root's black height.

Operations on Red-Black Trees: Operations on red-black

trees closely parallel those of AVL trees, encompassing both deletion and insertion, each accomplished in $(\log n) O(\log N)$ time for a tree with n keys. However, these operations necessitate adjustments to the red-black tree structure to uphold the defined properties. The primary operations include rotation, insertion, and deletion.

1. **Rotation:**

   - The rotation operation meticulously maintains the order of Ax by C.
   - Starting with a binary search tree and relying solely on rotation for restructuring ensures the preservation of the binary search tree property.
   - **Left Rotate (T, x):**

```
y ← right[x]
  right[x] ← left[y]
  p[left[y]] ← x
  p[y] ← p[x]

if p[x] = nil[T]
  then root[T] ← y
  else if x = left[p[x]]
  then left[p[x]] ← y
  else right[p[x]] ← y

left[y] ← x
  p[x] ← y
```
Insertion:

- New nodes are inserted akin to binary search trees, with the node initially colored red.
- Discrepancies in the tree, especially concerning parent and child nodes both being red, are rectified based on the node's position concerning the grandparent and the parent's sibling's color.
- **RB-INSERT (T, z):**

y ← nil[T]
  x ← root[T]

while x ≠ NIL[T]
  do y ← x
  if key[z] < key[x]
  then x ← left[x]
  else x ← right[x]

p[z] ← y
  if y = nil[T]
  then root[T] ← z
  else if key[z] < key[y]
  then left[y] ← z
  else right[y] ← z

left[z] ← nil[T]
  right[z] ← nil[T]
  color[z] ← RED

RB-INSERT-FIXUP (T, z)
Deletion:

- Node deletion involves multiple steps, including locating the element to be deleted and handling cases based on the node's children.
- If the deleted node is black, it might violate the black constraint, leading to potential violations of color constraints.
- **RB-DELETE (T, z):**

if left[z] = nil[T] or right[z] = nil[T]
  then y ← z
  else y ← TREE-SUCCESSOR(z)

if left[y] ≠ nil[T]
  then x ← left[y]
  else x ← right[y]

p[x] ← p[y]

if p[y] = nil[T]
  then root[T] ← x
  else if y = left[p[y]]
  then left[p[y]] ← x
  else right[p[y]] ← x

if y ≠ z
  then key[z] ← key[y]

if color[y] = BLACK
  then RB-DELETE-FIXUP(T, x)

return y

Maintaining Red-Black Tree Properties After Insertion:

After inserting a new node, coloring it black might violate black height conditions. Coloring it red could violate coloring constraints. The process is detailed in **RB-INSERT-FIXUP (T, z):** where color violations are rectified through cases involving rotations.

Maintaining Red-Black Tree Properties After Deletion: Deletion introduces potential violations of both black height and coloring constraints. The **RB-DELETE-FIXUP (T, x):** procedure is invoked after node splicing, ensuring the restoration of red-black properties by performing rotations and color adjustments based on specific cases.

In summary, red-black trees, with their nuanced approach to balancing, offer a sophisticated and efficient means of managing binary search trees while adhering to defined structural and coloring constraints.

Red-Black trees serve as self-balancing binary trees, devised by Rudolf Bayer in 1972. Each node in a red-black tree is assigned an additional attribute: a color, either red or black. These trees maintain balance by ensuring that the path from the root to any leaf node does not exceed twice the length of any other path, thus limiting the height to $O(logN)$, where N represents the number of nodes.

Key Characteristics:

1. The root node must always be black.
2. NIL nodes, representing leaf nodes, are considered black, ensuring that all non-NIL nodes have two children.
3. Children of red nodes must be black.
4. The black height rule mandates that for any node v, there

exists an integer bh(v) such that any path from v to a NIL node contains exactly bh(v) black nodes. The black height of the entire tree is determined by the root's black height.
5. Red-black trees are essentially variations of binary search trees.

Black Height:

The black height signifies the number of black nodes along the path from the root to a node, including leaf nodes. Thus, in a red-black tree with a height of h, the black height is at least h/2, ensuring that the number of nodes between a node and its farthest descendant (leaf) is no more than twice the number to the nearest descendant.

Regarding the height of red-black trees with n nodes, it can be proven that it is at most 2log2(n + 1) through the following steps:

1. In a standard binary tree, where k is the minimum number of nodes on all root-to-leaf paths, n is at least 2^k - 1. Equivalently, k is at most log2(n + 1).
2. In a red-black tree with n nodes, a root-to-leaf path contains at least log2(n + 1) black nodes.
3. As per the third property, the number of black nodes in the tree is at least |n/2|, where n represents the total number of nodes.

Hence, a red-black tree with n nodes has a height of at most 2log2(n + 1).

Below is a Java implementation demonstrating red-black tree traversal and insertion:

```java
// Import statements omitted

// Implementation of Red-Black Tree
  public class RedBlackTree {
  // Root node
  public Node root;

// Constructor for RedBlackTree
  public RedBlackTree() {
  super();
  root = null;
  }

// Node creation subclass
  class Node {
  int data;
  Node left;
  Node right;
  char color;
  Node parent;

// Constructor for Node
  Node(int data) {
  super();
  this.data = data;
  this.left = null;
  this.right = null;
  this.color = 'R';
```

```
        this.parent = null;
    }
}

// Left rotation operation
    Node rotateLeft(Node node) {
    Node x = node.right;
    Node y = x.left;
    x.left = node;
    node.right = y;
    node.parent = x;
    if (y != null)
    y.parent = node;
    return (x);
    }

// Right rotation operation
    Node rotateRight(Node node) {
    Node x = node.left;
    Node y = x.right;
    x.right = node;
    node.left = y;
    node.parent = x;
    if (y != null)
    y.parent = node;
    return (x);
    }

// Flags for rotation operations
    boolean ll = false;
    boolean rr = false;
```

```
boolean lr = false;
boolean rl = false;
```

```
// Helper function for insertion, handling all tasks in a single pass
    Node insertHelp(Node root, int data) {
    boolean f = false; // Flag for RED conflict
    if (root == null)
    return (new Node(data));
    else if (data < root.data) {
    root.left = insertHelp(root.left, data);
    root.left.parent = root;
    if (root != this.root) {
    if (root.color == 'R' && root.left.color == 'R')
    f = true;
    }
    } else {
    root.right = insertHelp(root.right, data);
    root.right.parent = root;
    if (root != this.root) {
    if (root.color == 'R' && root.right.color == 'R')
    f = true;
    }
    }

if (this.ll) {
   root = rotateLeft(root);
   root.color = 'B';
   root.left.color = 'R';
   this.ll = false;
   } else if (this.rr) {
```

```
        root = rotateRight(root);
        root.color = 'B';
        root.right.color = 'R';
        this.rr = false;
    } else if (this.rl) {
        root.right = rotateRight(root.right);
        root.right.parent = root;
        root = rotateLeft(root);
        root.color = 'B';
        root.left.color = 'R';
        this.rl = false;
    } else if (this.lr) {
        root.left = rotateLeft(root.left);
        root.left.parent = root;
        root = rotateRight(root);
        root.color = 'B';
        root.right.color = 'R';
        this.lr = false;
    }

if (f) {
    if (root.parent.right == root) {
        if (root.parent.left == null || root.parent.left.color == 'B') {
            if (root.left != null && root.left.color == 'R')
                this.rl = true;
            else if (root.right != null && root.right.color == 'R')
                this.ll = true;
        } else {
            root.parent.left.color = 'B';
            root.color = 'B';
            if (root.parent != this.root)
```

```
    root.parent.color = 'R';
    }
} else {
    if (root.parent.right == null || root.parent.right.color == 'B') {
    if (root.left != null && root.left.color == 'R')
    this.rr = true;
    else if (root.right != null && root.right.color == 'R')
    this.lr = true;
    } else {
    root.parent.right.color = 'B';
    root.color = 'B';
    if (root.parent != this.root)
    root.parent.color = 'R';
    }
    }
    f = false;
    }
    return (root);
    }

// Insert data into the tree
    public void insert(int data) {
    if (this.root == null) {
    this.root = new Node(data);
    this.root.color = 'B';
    } else
    this.root = insertHelp(this.root, data);
    }

// Helper function to print inorder traversal
    void inorderTraversalHelper(Node node) {
```

```java
        if (node != null) {
        inorderTraversalHelper(node.left);
        System.out.printf("%d ", node.data);
        inorderTraversalHelper(node.right);
        }
        }

    // Print inorder traversal of the tree
        public void inorderTraversal() {
        inorderTraversalHelper(this.root);
        }

    // Helper function to print the tree
        void printTreeHelper(Node root, int space) {
        int i;
        if (root != null) {
        space = space + 10;
        printTreeHelper(root.right, space);
        System.out.printf("\n");
        for (i = 10; i < space; i++) {
        System.out.printf(" ");
        }
        System.out.printf("%d", root.data);
        System.out.printf("\n");
        printTreeHelper(root.left, space);
        }
        }

    // Print the tree
        public void printTree() {
        printTreeHelper(this.root, 0);
```

}

```
public static void main(String[] args) {
    // Insert data into the tree, visualize, and traverse it
    RedBlackTree t = new RedBlackTree();
    int[] arr = {1, 4, 6, 3, 5, 7, 8, 2, 9};
    for (int i = 0; i < 9; i++) {
    t.insert(arr[i]);
    System.out.println();
    t.inorderTraversal();
    }
    // Check the color of any node using the attribute node.color
    t.printTree();
    }
}
```

The provided Java code implements a Red-Black Tree with insertion, rotation, and traversal functionalities. It uses flags to handle rotations and ensures the tree maintains the properties of a Red-Black Tree. The main method demonstrates tree insertion, traversal, and visualization.

Scapegoat Trees

Scapegoat Trees are a variant of self-balancing binary search trees, distinct from AVL and red-black trees in that they don't require additional node storage space. They are straightforward to implement and have minimal overhead, making them highly appealing data structures. Typically utilized in scenarios where lookup and insertion operations are frequent, their efficiency shines in these tasks.

The concept behind a scapegoat tree is akin to human behavior - when something goes awry, we often seek a scapegoat to assign blame. Similarly, in a scapegoat tree, after inserting a node, if it triggers an imbalance in the subtree, the scapegoat algorithm identifies the unbalanced node, termed the scapegoat, which then undergoes subtree rebalancing.

Scapegoat trees offer flexibility in implementation, allowing optimization for insertions, lookups, or deletions, catering to specific application requirements. Identifying a scapegoat node during insertion is a straightforward process - starting from the newly inserted node, the algorithm checks each node's subtree root until it discovers an unbalanced subtree, signifying the scapegoat.

Key properties of a scapegoat tree include size, root pointer, and max_size indicating the maximum tree size since the last complete rebuild. Each tree node holds properties such as key value, left and right child pointers.

In terms of operations, scapegoat trees handle insertion and deletion uniquely, while traversal and lookup follow standard binary search tree procedures.

Insertion

During insertion, after finding the appropriate position for the new node, the tree ascends the ancestry to locate the first node with an unbalanced subtree. While traversing up the tree has a time complexity of O(log2(n)), rebalancing the subtree rooted at the scapegoat takes O(n) time. However, amortized analysis suggests an O(log2(n)) time complexity.

Deletion

Deletion in scapegoat trees is simpler than insertion. The tree uses the max_size property to determine if a full rebalance is needed after deletion, ensuring an amortized time complexity similar to insertion.

In terms of complexity, scapegoat trees share similarities with other binary search trees but offer better space complexity, making them an attractive option for memory-constrained environments.

Python Implementation

Presented below is a Python implementation of the scapegoat tree, specifically focusing on the insert operation. It's important to note that for code clarity, each node maintains a pointer to its parent. However, this can be omitted by tracking parent nodes during tree traversal for stack insertion.

The code comprises two classes, namely the Node and the Scapegoat, each with their respective operations:

```python
import math

class Node:
    def __init__(self, key):
        self.key = key
```

```python
        self.left = None
        self.right = None
        self.parent = None

class Scapegoat:
    def __init__(self):
        self.root = None
        self.size = 0
        self.maxSize = 0

    def insert(self, key):
        node = Node(key)

        # Base Case - Nothing in the tree
        if self.root is None:
            self.root = node
            return

        # Search to find the correct place for the node
        currentNode = self.root
        while currentNode is not None:
            potentialParent = currentNode
            if node.key < currentNode.key:
                currentNode = currentNode.left
            else:
                currentNode = currentNode.right

        # Assign the new node with parents and siblings
        node.parent = potentialParent
        if node.key < node.parent.key:
            node.parent.left = node
```

```
    else:
    node.parent.right = node

node.left = None
    node.right = None
    self.size += 1
    scapegoat = self.findScapegoat(node)
    if scapegoat is None:
    return

tmp = self.rebalance(scapegoat)

# Assign the right pointers to and from the scapegoat
    scapegoat.left = tmp.left
    scapegoat.right = tmp.right
    scapegoat.key = tmp.key
    scapegoat.left.parent = scapegoat
    scapegoat.right.parent = scapegoat

def findScapegoat(self, node):
    if node == self.root:
    return None
    while self.isBalancedAtNode(node):
    if node == self.root:
    return None
    node = node.parent
    return node

def isBalancedAtNode(self, node):
    if abs(self.sizeOfSubtree(node.left) -
self.sizeOfSubtree(node.right))  <= 1:
```

```
        return True
    return False

def sizeOfSubtree(self, node):
    if node is None:
    return 0
    return 1 + self.sizeOfSubtree(node.left) + self.sizeOfSubtree(node.right)

def rebalance(self, root):
    def flatten(node, nodes):
    if node is None:
    return
    flatten(node.left, nodes)
    nodes.append(node)
    flatten(node.right, nodes)

def buildTreeFromSortedList(nodes, start, end):
    if start > end:
    return None
    mid = int(math.ceil(start + (end - start) / 2.0))
    node = Node(nodes[mid].key)
    node.left = buildTreeFromSortedList(nodes, start, mid-1)
    node.right = buildTreeFromSortedList(nodes, mid+1, end)
    return node

nodes = []
    flatten(root, nodes)
    return buildTreeFromSortedList(nodes, 0, len(nodes)-1)

def delete(self, key):
```

pass

The properties for both classes are defined in their constructors. Additionally, the parent pointer on line 6 aids in simplifying method writing.

Functions like **isBalancedAtNode** (lines 59 and 64) and **sizeOfSubtree** inform the insertion function about the scapegoat's location. **sizeOfSubtree** recursively explores the left and right paths beneath a node to count the number of nodes. **isBalancedAtTree** uses this information to identify whether a rooted subtree at a specified node is balanced or not.

The insertion function (line 15) is crucial. After placing the new node at the tree's bottom, backtracking is done to find the scapegoat by following parent pointers. The **findScapegoat** function (line 50) manages this, and when the while loop (line 53) fails due to an absence of a balanced subtree beneath the inspected node, indicating the need for tree rebalancing.

The function to rebalance the tree (line 69) involves recursively flattening the tree into a sorted list. Subsequently, a binary search creates a new balanced tree, which is then reconnected to the original tree using the code on lines 44 to 48.

Although the delete function isn't included, its logic aligns with insertion, with the advantage that the scapegoat will always be the root node.

Treap

Similar to a binary search tree, a treap exhibits distinct characteristics. It lacks a guaranteed height of O(logN), relying instead on binary heap and randomization properties to maintain balance with high probability. Expected time complexities for insert, delete, and search functions are O(logN).

Each node in a treap holds two values:

1. Key: Follows the ordering in a standard binary search tree, with the right being greater and the left smaller.
2. Priority: A randomly assigned value following the Max-Heap property.

Basic Operations

Aligned with other self-balancing trees, the treap upholds the Max-Heap property during insertion and deletion through rotations. In the example below, T1, T2, and T3 represent subtrees of the left-rooted tree with y or the right-rooted tree with x:

```
   y                            x
  / \    Right Rotation        / \
 x  T3  - - - - - - - ->     T1  y
 / \    <- - - - - - -           / \
T1 T2    Left Rotation         T2 T3
```

In both trees, the keys follow the order: keys(T1) < key(x) < keys(T2) < key(y) < keys(T3), ensuring adherence to the binary search tree property.

Search

Searching in a treap tree mirrors the process in any standard binary search tree, requiring no additional explanation.

Insert

Inserting a new node involves these steps:

1. Create a new node with key = x and value = a random value.
2. Follow a standard binary search tree insert procedure.
3. Perform rotations to ensure that the priority for the newly inserted node adheres to the Max-Heap property.

Delete

To delete a node, follow these steps:

1. Check if the node to delete is a leaf; if yes, delete it.
2. If the node is not a leaf, replace the priority with -INF (minus infinite), and bring the node down to a leaf by executing right rotations.

Implementing the Operations:

```
// C++ function for searching a specified key in a given binary search tree
TreapNode* search(TreapNode* root, int key)
{
// Base Cases: the root is null or the key is present at the root
if (root == NULL || root->key == key)
return root;
// The key is greater than the root's key
if (root->key < key)
return search(root->right, key);
// The key is smaller than the root's key
return search(root->left, key);
}
```

Insert

1. Create a new node with key = x and the value = a random value.
2. Perform a standard binary search tree insert.
3. When a new node is inserted, assign it a random priority, which may violate the Max-Heap property. To ensure the priority follows Max-Heap, perform right rotations.
4. Upon node insertion, recursively traverse all its ancestors:

a. If the node is inserted in the left subtree and the left subtree's root has a higher priority, perform a right rotation.

b. If the node is inserted in the right subtree and the right subtree's root has a higher priority, perform a left rotation.

Here is a recursive implementation of the insertion operation in a treap:

```cpp
TreapNode* insert(TreapNode* root, int key)
{
// If the root is NULL, create a new node and return it
if (!root)
return newNode(key);
// If the key is smaller than the root
if (key <= root->key)
{
// Insert in the left subtree
root->left = insert(root->left, key);
// Fix the Heap property if it is violated
if (root->left->priority > root->priority)
root = rightRotate(root);
}
```

```
else // If the key is greater
{
// Insert in the right subtree
root->right = insert(root->right, key);
// Fix the Heap property if it is violated
if (root->right->priority > root->priority)
root = leftRotate(root);
}
return root;
}
```

Delete This implementation differs slightly from the previous one:

1. Check if the node you want to delete is a leaf – if yes, delete it.
2. If the node has a NULL and a NON-NULL child, replace the node with the NON-NULL child.
3. If both of the node's children are NON-NULL, find the maximum priority among the left and right children: a. If the right child's priority is greater, perform a left rotation at the node. b. If the left child's priority is greater, perform a right rotation at the node.

The objective of the third step is to move the node down to end up with a situation similar to either a or b.

Below is a recursive implementation of the Delete operation:

```
TreapNode* deleteNode(TreapNode* root, int key)
{
// Base case
if (root == NULL) return root;
// If the key is not at the root
```

```
if (key < root->key)
    root->left = deleteNode(root->left, key);
else if (key > root->key)
    root->right = deleteNode(root->right, key);
// If the key is at the root
// If the left is NULL
else if (root->left == NULL)
{
    TreapNode *temp = root->right;
    delete(root);
    root = temp; // Make the right child as root
}
// If the Right is NULL
else if (root->right == NULL)
{
    TreapNode *temp = root->left;
    delete(root);
    root = temp; // Make the left child as root
}
// If the key is at the root and both the left and right are not NULL
else if (root->left->priority < root->right->priority)
{
    root = leftRotate(root);
    root->left = deleteNode(root->left, key);
}
else
{
    root = rightRotate(root);
    root->right = deleteNode(root->right, key);
}
```

return root;
}

The complete program in C++ demonstrating all the operations and the output:

```cpp
// C++ program demonstrating search, insert, and delete in Treap
#include
using namespace std;

// A Treap Node
struct TreapNode
{
    int key, priority;
    TreapNode *left, *right;
};

// Right rotation of the subtree rooted with y
TreapNode *rightRotate(TreapNode *y)
{
    TreapNode *x = y->left, *T2 = x->right;
    // Perform rotation
    x->right = y;
    y->left = T2;
    // Return the new root
    return x;
}

// Left rotation of the subtree rooted with x
TreapNode *leftRotate(TreapNode *x)
{
    TreapNode *y = x->right, *T2 = y->left;
```

```
// Perform the rotation
y->left = x;
x->right = T2;
// Return the new root
return y;
}


// Utility function to add a new key
    TreapNode* newNode(int key)
    {
    TreapNode* temp = new TreapNode;
    temp->key = key;
    temp->priority = rand()%100;
    temp->left = temp->right = NULL;
    return temp;
    }


// C function to search a specified key in a specified binary search tree
    TreapNode* search(TreapNode* root, int key)
    {
    // Base Cases: the root is null or key is present at the root
    if (root == NULL || root->key == key)
    return root;
    // The key is greater than the root's key
    if (root->key < key)
    return search(root->right, key);
    // The key is smaller than the root's key
    return search(root->left, key);
    }
```

```
// Recursive implementation of insertion in Treap
TreapNode* insert(TreapNode* root, int key)
{
    // If the root is NULL, create a new node and return it
    if (!root)
        return newNode(key);
    // If the key is smaller than the root
    if (key <= root->key)
    {
        // Insert in the left subtree
        root->left = insert(root->left, key);
        // Fix the Heap property if it is violated
        if (root->left->priority > root->priority)
            root = rightRotate(root);
    }
    else // If the key is greater
    {
        // Insert in the right subtree
        root->right = insert(root->right, key);
        // Fix the Heap property if it is violated
        if (root->right->priority > root->priority)
            root = leftRotate(root);
    }
    return root;
}

// Recursive implementation of Delete()
TreapNode* deleteNode(TreapNode* root, int key)
{
    if (root == NULL)
        return root;
```

```
if (key < root->key)
root->left = deleteNode(root->left, key);
else if (key > root->key)
root->right = deleteNode(root->right, key);
// If the key is at the root
// If the left is NULL
else if (root->left == NULL)
{
TreapNode *temp = root->right;
delete(root);
root = temp; // Make the right child as root
}
// If the Right is NULL
else if (root->right == NULL)
{
TreapNode *temp = root->left;
delete(root);
root = temp; // Make the left child as root
}
// If the key is at the root and both the left and right are not NULL
  else if (root->left->priority < root->right->priority)
  {
  root = leftRotate(root);
  root->left = deleteNode(root->left, key);
  }
  else
  {
  root = rightRotate(root);
  root->right = deleteNode(root->right, key);
  }
```

```
    return root;
}

// Utility function to print the tree
void inorder(TreapNode* root)
{
    if (root)
    {
        inorder(root->left);
        cout << "key: "<< root->key << " | priority: %d "
        << root->priority;
        if (root->left)
        cout << " | left child: " << root->left->key;
        if (root->right)
        cout << " | right child: " << root->right->key;
        cout << endl;
        inorder(root->right);
    }
}

// Driver Program to test these functions
int main()
{
    srand(time(NULL));
    struct TreapNode *root = NULL;
    root = insert(root, 50);
    root = insert(root, 30);
    root = insert(root, 20);
    root = insert(root, 40);
    root = insert(root, 70);
    root = insert(root, 60);
```

```
root = insert(root, 80);
cout << "Inorder traversal of the specified tree \n";
inorder(root);
cout << "\nDelete 20\n";
root = deleteNode(root, 20);
cout << "Inorder traversal of the newly modified tree \n";
inorder(root);
cout << "\nDelete 30\n";
root = deleteNode(root, 30);
cout << "Inorder traversal of the newly modified tree \n";
inorder(root);
cout << "\nDelete 50\n";
root = deleteNode(root, 50);
cout << "Inorder traversal of the newly modified tree \n";
inorder(root);
TreapNode *res = search(root, 50);
(res == NULL)? cout << "\n50 Not Found ":
cout << "\n50 found";
return 0;
}
```

Output:

Inorder traversal of the specified tree key: 20 | priority: %d 92 | right child: 50 key: 30 | priority: %d 48 | right child: 40 key: 40 | priority: %d 21 key: 50 | priority: %d 73 | left child: 30 | right child: 60 key: 60 | priority: %d 55 | right child: 70 key: 70 | priority: %d 50 | right child: 80 key: 80 | priority: %d 44 Delete 20 Inorder traversal of the newly modified tree key: 30 | priority: %d 48 | right child: 40 key: 40 | priority: %d 21 key: 50 | priority: %d 73 | left child: 30 | right child: 60 key: 60 |

priority: %d 55 | right child: 70 key: 70 | priority: %d 50 | right child: 80 key: 80 | priority: %d 44 Delete 30 Inorder traversal of the newly modified tree key: 40 | priority: %d 21 key: 50 | priority: %d 73 | left child: 40 | right child: 60 key: 60 | priority: %d 55 | right child: 70 key: 70 | priority: %d 50 | right child: 80 key: 80 | priority: %d 44 Delete 50 Inorder traversal of the newly modified tree key: 40 | priority: %d 21 key: 60 | priority: %d 55 | left child: 40 | right child: 70 key: 70 | priority: %d 50 | right child: 80 key: 80 | priority: %d 44 50

Explanation of the Output:
The nodes are represented as key(priority), and the provided code generates the following tree:
20(92)
\
50(73)
/ \
30(48) 60(55)
\ \
40(21) 70(50)
\
80(44)
After executing the deleteNode(20) operation:
50(73)
/ \
30(48) 60(55)
\ \
40(21) 70(50)
\
80(44)
After executing the deleteNode(30) operation:

```
50(73)
/ \
40(21) 60(55)
      \
      70(50)
            \
            80(44)
```

After executing the deleteNode(50) operation:

```
60(55)
/ \
40(21) 70(50)
            \
            80(44)
```

This series of operations demonstrates the deletion of nodes 20, 30, and 50 from the original tree, resulting in the modified tree structures as shown.

N-ary Tree

The term "N-ary tree" is coined due to the ability of a node to have n-number of children, distinguishing it from standard binary search trees where nodes can only have up to two children. A visual representation of an N-ary tree reveals its complexity, with some nodes having three children while others have just one. In contrast to binary trees, where child nodes are conveniently stored as left and right nodes, N-ary trees require a different data structure. In Java, a LinkedList is used, and in C++, a vector.

Implementation:

Implementation of an N-ary tree begins with the creation of a structure (in Java, a constructor) for the data structure. Similar to a binary search tree, the TreeNode class is employed, and constructors are established within it, incorporating class-level variables.

Consider the following example:

```
public static class TreeNode {
int val;
List children = new LinkedList<>();

TreeNode(int data) {
  val = data;
  }

TreeNode(int data, List child) {
  val = data;
  children = child;
  }
}
```

The TreeNode class features two overloaded constructors, sharing the same name but with different parameters. "Val" stores a node's value, while "List" stores the node's children nodes.

This code provides the foundational structure of an N-ary tree, requiring the construction of the tree and subsequent utilization of level-order traversal for printing. The defined constructors are employed to build the tree

```
public static void main(String[] args) {
```

```
// Creating a replica of the N-ary Tree
TreeNode root = new TreeNode(1);
root.children.add(new TreeNode(2));
root.children.add(new TreeNode(3));
root.children.add(new TreeNode(4));
root.children.get(0).children.add(new TreeNode(5));
root.children.get(0).children.add(new TreeNode(6));
root.children.get(0).children.add(new TreeNode(7));
root.children.get(1).children.add(new TreeNode(8));
root.children.get(2).children.add(new TreeNode(9));
root.children.get(2).children.add(new TreeNode(10));
root.children.get(2).children.add(new TreeNode(11));
printNAryTree(root);
}
```

The root node of the N-ary tree is initially created, and children are assigned to the root node using the dot operator and accessing the root node's children property. The "add()" method from the List interface is utilized to add children to the root nodes.

Subsequently, the children of all level nodes are added by using the "get()" method from the List interface to access the node and add the appropriate children.

Finally, the "printNAryTree" method is invoked to print the tree.

While printing trees might seem straightforward, it involves the use of different algorithms rather than a simple loop through a series of items. Algorithms such as Inorder Traversal, Preorder Traversal, PostOrder Traversal, and Level Order Traversal are employed. For simplicity, Level Order Traversal is chosen here, assuming prior familiarity with its application in binary search trees.

Level Order Traversal

Level Order Traversal prioritizes printing nodes at the root level before progressing to the subsequent levels, continuing until the final level is reached. The nodes are organized at each level through the utilization of the Queue data structure.

Consider the example tree below:

For this tree, Level Order Traversal produces the following output:

1
2 3 4 5

Examine the provided code:

```
private static void printNAryTree(TreeNode root){
    if(root == null) return;
    Queue queue = new LinkedList<>();
    queue.offer(root);
    while(!queue.isEmpty()) {
    int len = queue.size();
    for(int i=0;i
    TreeNode node = queue.poll();
    System.out.print(node.val + " ");
    for (TreeNode item : node.children) { // for-Each loop will iterate over all the children
    queue.offer(item);
    }
    }
    System.out.println();
    }
```

}

The entire code is as follows:

```java
import java.util.LinkedList;
import java.util.List;
import java.util.Queue;

public class NAryTree {
    public static class TreeNode{
        int val;
        List children = new LinkedList<>();

        TreeNode(int data){
            val = data;
        }

        TreeNode(int data,List child){
            val = data;
            children = child;
        }
    }

    private static void printNAryTree(TreeNode root){
        if(root == null) return;
        Queue queue = new LinkedList<>();
        queue.offer(root);
        while(!queue.isEmpty()) {
            int len = queue.size();
            for(int i=0;i
            TreeNode node = queue.poll();
            assert node != null;
            System.out.print(node.val + " ");
```

```
      for (TreeNode item : node.children) {
        queue.offer(item);
      }
    }
    System.out.println();
  }
}

public static void main(String[] args) {
  TreeNode root = new TreeNode(1);
  root.children.add(new TreeNode(2));
  root.children.add(new TreeNodc(3));
  root.children.add(new TreeNode(4));
  root.children.get(0).children.add(new TreeNode(5));
  root.children.get(0).children.add(new TreeNode(6));
  root.children.get(0).children.add(new TreeNode(7));
  root.children.get(1).children.add(new TreeNode(8));
  root.children.get(2).children.add(new TreeNode(9));
  root.children.get(2).children.add(new TreeNode(10));
  root.children.get(2).children.add(new TreeNode(11));
  printNAryTree(root);
  }
}
```

The output of this code is as follows:

1
2 3 4
5 6 7 8 9 10 11

This output corresponds to the N-ary tree shown initially, with each level node retaining the same values.

Varieties of N-ary Trees

There are several types of N-ary trees to be familiar with:

Complete N-ary

1. Tree In a Complete N-ary Tree, a node is allowed to have either N children or none at all.

Full N-ary

2. Tree A Complete N-ary Tree requires that each node at every level has exactly N children, ensuring completeness. The only exception is the last level nodes, which, if incomplete, should be "as left as possible."

Perfect N-ary

3.Tree Perfect N-ary Trees are characterized by being full trees, with all leaf node levels being uniform.

4

PART 3 : Disjoint Sets

Disjoint-Set Data Structures

In the realm of computer science, a data structure recognized as a disjoint-set, merge-find set, or union-find structure plays a pivotal role. These structures manage collections of disjoint sets, which are essentially non-overlapping sets. Within each disjoint subset, a partition of a set is stored. These structures offer essential operations such as adding new sets, merging sets, and identifying representative set members. The latter operation provides an efficient means to determine whether two elements share a set or belong to distinct ones.

Various implementations of disjoint-set data structures exist, but the prevailing approach involves using a disjoint-set forest. These specialized forests facilitate near-constant amortized time for union and find operations. When a sequence of m addition, find, or union operations is executed with n nodes on a disjoint-set data structure, the overall time required is $O(m\alpha(n))$, where $\alpha(n)$ denotes the inverse Ackermann function—an exceedingly slow-growing function.

It is important to note that while the disjoint-set forest may not guarantee consistent performance on a per-operation basis, individual operations prompt the forest to adapt, enhancing subsequent operations' speed. Disjoint-set forests are not only efficient but also asymptotically optimal.

These data structures play a crucial role in algorithms like Kruskal's, designed to identify the minimum spanning tree of a graph. Due to their significance, disjoint-set structures find applications in various algorithms.

Structure Representation:

In a disjoint-set forest, each node possesses two attributes: a pointer and supplementary information, typically a rank or size, but never both. Pointers are employed to create parent pointer trees, where a non-root node points to its parent node. Invalid values, such as sentinel values or circular references, are used in parent pointers to distinguish them easily from other nodes.

Each tree in the forest represents a set, with tree nodes serving as the set members. The root node functions as the set representative, and two nodes can share a set if their tree roots are equal. Nodes can be stored in the forest in diverse ways, with one common technique being the use of arrays. In this approach, array indices denote the parents, and each array entry requires $\Theta(\log n)$ bits for parent pointers, contributing to a total storage of $\Theta(n \log n)$ bits. If fixed-size nodes limit the forest to a maximum storage size, linear storage proportional to n is considered appropriate.

Operations:

Disjoint-set data structures support three fundamental operations:

1. Creating new sets with new elements
2. Locating the set's representative with a specified element
3. Merging two sets

These operations collectively form the foundation of disjoint-set data structure functionality.

Establishing New Sets

The addition of new elements is accomplished through the MakeSet operation. This operation involves placing the new element into a fresh set containing just that single element, subsequently incorporating this set into the disjoint-set data structure. From a perspective of viewing the structure as a partition of a set, the MakeSet operation enlarges the set, extending the partition by introducing the element into a new subset comprising a solitary element—the newly added one.

In the context of the disjoint-set forest, this operation initializes the parent pointer and either the size or rank of the node. Utilizing pseudocode, if a node pointing to itself denotes the root, the addition of a new element can be expressed as follows:

```
function MakeSet(x) is
    if x is not in the forest already, then
    x.parent := x
    x.size := 1 // if nodes store size
    x.rank := 0 // if nodes store rank
    end if
end function
```

The time complexity for this operation is constant, and when initializing a forest with n nodes, it requires $O(n)$ time. In practice, preceding the MakeSet operation with another operation for memory allocation, holding x, is necessary. The asymptotic performance of the disjoint-set forest remains consistent as long as the memory allocation operation occurs in amortized constant time, similar to implementing a dynamic array.

Identifying a Representative

The Find operation entails traversing a specific path—from the given query node x, it follows a series of parent pointers until reaching a root element. This root element serves as the representative of the set to which x belongs. The Find operation returns the root element.

Optimizing the forest involves flattening the tree during the Find operation, reducing the time required. Flattening the tree entails updating parent pointers so that they point closer to the root. Although the sets stored in the forest remain unchanged, this optimization accelerates successive Find operations for nodes between the root and the query point and all their descendants. The amortized performance guarantee relies on this updating.

Various algorithms for the Find operation achieve asymptotically optimal time complexity. Path compression, a family of algorithms, compresses all nodes between the root and the query point to the root. Path compression can be implemented using recursion:

```
function Find(x) is
    if x.parent ≠ x then
        x.parent := Find(x.parent)
        return x.parent
    else
        return x
    end if
end function
```

The implementation involves two passes—up the tree and back down. Adequate scratch memory is necessary to store the path between the query and root nodes. Alternatively, one-pass Find algorithms like path halving and path splitting are more efficient, updating parent pointers for nodes on the path from the query to the root node. Path splitting replaces all parent pointers on the path with a pointer to the grandparent, while path halving only replaces every alternate parent pointer.

Combining Two Sets

The Union(x, y) operation involves merging two sets – one with x and the other with y – into a unified set. This process utilizes the Find operation to identify the roots in the trees containing x and y. If the roots are identical, no further action is needed. However, if the roots differ, the subsequent step is to merge the trees, achieved by setting either x's root pointer to y's or vice versa. The choice of the parent node can impact the future complexity of tree operations, as an incautious choice may result in an overly tall tree.

To manage tree height efficiently, implementations often employ Union by Rank or Union by Size. Both methods necessitate nodes storing a parent pointer along with additional information, determining the parent root. These approaches prevent the formation of excessively deep trees.

In Union by Size, the node's size, representing the count of descendants, is stored within the node. When merging trees with x and y roots, the parent node is the one with the greater number of descendants. If both nodes have equal descendants, either can be the parent, with the parent node set to the total descendant count:

```
function Union(x, y) is
// Replace nodes by roots
x := Find(x)
y := Find(y)
if x = y then
return // x and y are already in the same set
end if
// If needed, rename the variables to ensure that
// x has at least as many descendants as y
if x.size < y.size then
```

(x, y) := (y, x)
end if
// Make x the new root
y.parent := x
// Update the size of x
x.size := x.size + y.size
end function

The number of bits needed to store node size aligns with the number needed for n, providing the necessary storage with a constant factor.

In Union by Rank, the node's rank, representing the upper bound of height, is stored within the node. When merging trees with x and y roots, their ranks are compared. If unequal, the larger rank becomes the parent, leaving x and y ranks unchanged. If ranks are equal, either can be the parent, but the parent's rank increases by 1. Storing ranks proves more efficient during Find operations, where a node's height may change, eliminating the extra work required to maintain correct height.

function Union(x, y) is
// Replace nodes by roots
x := Find(x)
y := Find(y)
if x = y then
return // x and y are in the same set
end if
// If needed, rename the variables to ensure that
// x has rank at least as large as that of y
if x.rank < y.rank then
(x, y) := (y, x)
end if

```
// Make x the new root
y.parent := x
// If needed, increment the rank of x
if x.rank = y.rank then
x.rank := x.rank + 1
end if
end function
```

Nodes have ranks of (logN) or lower, and storing ranks requires O(log log n) bits, making it asymptotically negligible in the overall forest size.

These implementations highlight that node rank and size are irrelevant once the node becomes a tree root. As a child, access to its size and rank is never required.

Time Complexity

Disjoint-set forest implementations without parent pointer updates by the Find operation and lacking Union-induced tree height control may harbor trees with O(n) height, demanding O(n) time.

For implementations using only path compression, the worst-case running time of a sequence involving n MakeSet operations, no more than n − 1 Union operations, and f Find operations is θ(n + f . (1 + log 2+f/n n)).

In Union by Rank, with no parent pointer updates during the Find operation, the running time for m operations up to n (MakeSet operations) ranges from θ(m log n) to θ(mα(n)). Each operation maintains an amortized running time of θ(α(n)), achieving asymptotic optimality and ensuring Ω(α(n)) for every disjoint-set operation. The inverse Ackerman function, α(n), grows exceptionally slowly, with a factor of 4 or lower for any n in the physical universe, granting amortized constant time for all disjoint-set operations.

5

PART 4 :Advanced Heapsand Priority Queues

Binary Heap vs. Binary Search Tree for Priority Queues

When it comes to priority queues, binary heaps consistently stand out as the preferred choice over binary search trees. Efficiency in a priority queue is contingent upon four essential operations:

1. Retrieve the minimum or maximum to ascertain the top-priority element.
2. Insert an element.
3. Remove the top-priority element.
4. Decrease the key.

Binary heaps excel in supporting these operations with the following time complexities:

1. O(1)
2. O(Logn)
3. O(Logn)
4. O(Logn)

These operations, with the same time complexities, are also supported by red-black trees, AVL trees, and other self-balancing binary search trees.

Let's delve into the breakdown of these operations:

1. Achieving O(1) for finding the minimum and maximum isn't inherently natural. However, by maintaining an additional pointer to the min or max and updating it during deletion or insertion as necessary, this complexity can be achieved. Deletion triggers an update through finding the inorder successor or predecessor.

2. O(Logn) is the inherent time complexity for inserting elements.

3. O(Logn) is likewise the natural complexity for removing the minimum and maximum.

4. Decreasing the key can be accomplished in O(Logn) through a sequence of deletion and insertion.

Now, how does this preference for binary heaps address the fundamental question? The answer lies in the use of arrays to implement binary heaps, ensuring superior locality of reference and more cache-friendly operations.

Despite the shared time complexities, binary search trees consistently incur higher constants. Building a binary heap takes $O(n)$ time, whereas a self-balancing binary search tree necessitates $O(nLogn)$ time. Binary heaps, unlike binary search trees, don't require additional space for pointers, making them more efficient in terms of memory usage. Moreover, implementing binary heaps is significantly easier than binary search trees.

Various iterations of binary heaps, such as the Fibonacci Heap supporting insert and decrease-key operations in $\theta(1)$ time, further enhance their versatility.

Yet, it's crucial to acknowledge that while binary heaps excel in priority queues, binary search trees offer a broader array of advantages. For instance:

- Searching for an element in a self-balancing binary search tree takes $O(Logn)$ time, whereas in a binary heap, it takes $O(n)$ time.
 - Printing all elements in sorted order is more efficient in a binary search tree ($O(n)$) compared to a binary heap ($O(nLogn)$).
 - Introducing an additional field to a binary search tree allows fetching the kth smallest or largest element in $O(Logn)$ time.

In summary, the supremacy of binary heaps in priority queues is clear, but exploring the diverse advantages of binary search trees unveils a nuanced landscape.

Binomial Heap: Enhancing Priority Queue Efficiency

Binary heaps serve a pivotal role, primarily in the implementation of priority queues. The binomial heap, an extension of the binary heap, not only embraces all the functionalities of a binary heap but also introduces significantly faster merge or union operations.

So, what defines a binomial heap? Let's envision a binomial tree with an order of 0 – a lone node. Constructing a binomial tree with an order 'k' involves two binomial trees of order 'k-1,' with one set as the left child. This 'k' ordered tree has distinctive properties:

- It boasts precisely 2^k nodes.
    - Its depth is 'k.'
    - At depth 'i' (ranging from 0 to 'k'), it exactly has 'k choose i' nodes.

The root of this tree holds a degree of 'k,' and its children are binomial trees with descending orders from 'k-1' to '0.'

Let's explore the binomial heap, which essentially comprises a sequence of binomial trees. Each tree adheres to the Min Heap property, ensuring that at most one tree of any particular degree exists. Illustrative examples showcase a binomial heap with 13 nodes, comprising three trees with orders 0, 2, and 3, as well as a heap with 12 nodes, consisting of two trees with orders 2 and 3.

Representing numbers and binomial heaps in binary involves a fascinating connection. If a binomial heap has 'n' nodes, the number of binomial trees aligns with the set bits in 'n's binary representation. For instance, if 'n' is 13 with a binary representation of 00001101 (three set bits), there are three binomial trees. The degrees of these trees correlate with the positions of the set bits, leading to the conclusion that a binomial heap with 'n' nodes encompasses O(Logn) binomial trees.

Now, let's delve into the operations of the binomial heap:

1. **insert(H, k):** This operation inserts the key 'k' into the binomial heap 'H,' creating a heap with a single key. Subsequently, the union operation is invoked on 'H' and the newly formed binomial heap.

2. **getMin(H):** Obtaining the minimum involves traversing the root list of trees and returning the smallest key. While this typically requires O(Logn) time, optimization to O(1) is achievable by maintaining a pointer to the minimum key root.

3. **extractMin(H):** This operation also leverages the union operation. Initially, getMin() is called to obtain the minimum key tree. Following this, the node is removed, and a new binomial heap forms by connecting all subtrees from the removed node. Finally, union() is invoked on 'H' and the new

heap. This entire process operates within O(Logn) time.

4. delete(H): Similar to the binary heap, the delete operation involves reducing the key to negative infinity and subsequently calling extractMin().

5. decreaseKey(H):Resembling the binary heap, this operation compares the decreased key with its parent. If the parent key is greater, a swap ensues, and the process recurs for the parent key. This continues until reaching a node where the parent key is smaller or reaching the root node. decreaseKey() has a time complexity of O(Logn).

Combining Binomial Heaps: The Union Process

Imagine having two binomial heaps, named H1 and H2. Employing the union() operation, these heaps merge into a single binomial heap through the following steps:

1. Initially, the heaps are merged by arranging them in non-decreasing order based on their degrees.
2. After merging, it's imperative to ensure there's no more than one binomial tree of any degree. This necessitates combining binomial trees with identical orders. The process involves traversing the list of merged roots while tracking three pointers: prev, x, and next-x. Several scenarios are encountered during this traversal: i. If the orders of x and next-x differ, no further action is taken. ii. If the order of next-next-x matches that of x, the traversal proceeds. iii. When the key of x is equal to or less than the

key of next-x, next-x becomes a child of x, establishing a link between them. iv. If the key of x is greater than that of next-x, x becomes the child of next.

Implementation of Binomial Heap in C++

The subsequent C++ code illustrates the execution of fundamental operations like insert(), getMin(), and extractMin() on a Binomial Heap:

```cpp
// C++ program to implement some operations
// on Binomial Heap
#include
using namespace std;

// Definition of a Binomial Tree node
struct Node
{
int data, degree;
Node *child, *sibling, *parent;
};

// Function to create a new node
Node* newNode(int key)
{
Node *temp = new Node;
temp->data = key;
temp->degree = 0;
temp->child = temp->parent = temp->sibling = NULL;
return temp;
}
```

```cpp
// Function to merge two Binomial Trees
Node* mergeBinomialTrees(Node *b1, Node *b2)
{
    // b1 must be smaller
    if (b1->data > b2->data)
        swap(b1, b2);
    // Set a larger valued tree
    // as a child of a tree with a smaller value
    b2->parent = b1;
    b2->sibling = b1->child;
    b1->child = b2;
    b1->degree++;
    return b1;
}


// Function to perform the union operation on
// two binomial heaps l1 & l2
list unionBionomialHeap(list l1,
list l2)
{
    // _new to another binomial heap with a
    // new heap after merging l1 & l2
    list _new;
    list::iterator it = l1.begin();
    list::iterator ot = l2.begin();
    while (it!=l1.end() && ot!=l2.end())
    {
        // if D(l1) <= D(l2)
        if((*it)->degree <= (*ot)->degree)
        {
            _new.push_back(*it);
```

```
        it++;
    }
    // if D(l1) > D(l2)
    else
    {
        _new.push_back(*ot);
        ot++;
    }
}
// if some elements remain in l1
// binomial heap
while (it != l1.end())
{
    _new.push_back(*it);
    it++;
}
// if some elements remain in l2
// binomial heap
while (ot!=l2.end())
{
    _new.push_back(*ot);
    ot++;
}
return _new;
}

// Function to rearrange the heap so that
    // the heap is in increasing order of degree and
    // no two binomial trees have the same degree in this heap
    list adjust(list _heap)
    {
```

```cpp
if (_heap.size() <= 1)
return _heap;
list new_heap;
list::iterator it1,it2,it3;
it1 = it2 = it3 = _heap.begin();
if (_heap.size() == 2)
{
it2 = it1;
it2++;
it3 = _heap.end();
}
else
{
it2++;
it3=it2;
it3++;
}
while (it1 != _heap.end())
{
// if only a single element remains to be processed
if (it2 == _heap.end())
it1++;
// If D(it1) < D(it2) i.e. merging of Binomial
// Tree pointed by it1 & it2 is not possible
// then move next in heap
else if ((*it1)->degree < (*it2)->degree)
{
it1++;
it2++;
if(it3!=_heap.end())
it3++;
```

```
    }
    // if D(it1),D(it2) & D(it3) are same i.e.
    // degree of three consecutive Binomial Tree are same
    // in heap
    else if (it3!=_heap.end() &&
    (*it1)->degree == (*it2)->degree &&
    (*it1)->degree == (*it3)->degree)
    {
    it1++;
    it2++;
    it3++;
    }
    // if the degrees of two Binomial Trees are the same in the heap
    else if ((*it1)->degree == (*it2)->degree)
    {
    Node *temp;
    *it1 = mergeBinomialTrees(*it1,*it2);
    it2 = _heap.erase(it2);
    if(it3 != _heap.end())
    it3++;
    }
    }
    return _heap;
    }

// Function to insert a Binomial Tree into a binomial heap
    list insertATreeInHeap(list _heap,
    Node *tree)
    {
    // creating a new heap i.e temp
```

```
list temp;
// inserting Binomial Tree into heap
temp.push_back(tree);
// perform union operation to finally insert
// Binomial Tree in original heap
temp = unionBionomialHeap(_heap,temp);
return adjust(temp);
}


// Function to remove the minimum key element from the binomial heap
// this function takes the Binomial Tree as an input and returns
// a binomial heap after
// removing the head of that tree, i.e., minimum element
list removeMinFromTreeReturnBHeap(Node *tree)
{
list heap;
Node *temp = tree->child;
Node *lo;
// creating a binomial heap from Binomial Tree
while (temp)
{
lo = temp;
temp = temp->sibling;
lo->sibling = NULL;
heap.push_front(lo);
}
return heap;
}
```

```cpp
// Function to insert a key into the binomial heap
list insert(list _head, int key)
{
    Node *temp = newNode(key);
    return insertATreeInHeap(_head,temp);
}

// Function to return a pointer of the minimum value Node
// present in the binomial heap
Node* getMin(list _heap)
{
    list::iterator it = _heap.begin();
    Node *temp = *it;
    while (it != _heap.end())
    {
        if ((*it)->data < temp->data)
            temp = *it;
        it++;
    }
    return temp;
}

list extractMin(list _heap)
{
    list new_heap,lo;
    Node *temp;
    // temp contains the pointer of the minimum value
    // element in heap
    temp = getMin(_heap);
    list::iterator it;
    it = _heap.begin();
```

```
while (it != _heap.end())
{
if (*it != temp)
{
// inserting all Binomial Tree into new
// binomial heap except the Binomial Tree
// contains minimum element
new_heap.push_back(*it);
}
it++;
}
lo = removeMinFromTreeReturnBHeap(temp);
new_heap = unionBionomialHeap(new_heap,lo);
new_heap = adjust(new_heap);
return new_heap;
}

// Function to print a Binomial Tree
void printTree(Node *h)
{
while (h)
{
cout « h->data « " ";
printTree(h->child);
h = h->sibling;
}
}

// Function to print a binomial heap
void printHeap(list _heap)
{
```

```
list ::iterator it;
it = _heap.begin();
while (it != _heap.end())
{
printTree(*it);
it++;
}
}
```

```
// Driver program to test above functions
int main()
{
int ch,key;
list _heap;
// Insert data in the heap
_heap = insert(_heap,10);
_heap = insert(_heap,20);
_heap = insert(_heap,30);
cout << "Heap elements after insertion:\n";
printHeap(_heap);
Node *temp = getMin(_heap);
cout << "\nMinimum element of heap "
<< temp->data << "\n";
// Delete minimum element of heap
_heap = extractMin(_heap);
cout << "Heap after deletion of minimum element\n";
printHeap(_heap);
return 0;
}
```

Output: The heap is: 50 10 30 40 20 After deleting 10, the heap is: 20 30 40 50

Fibonacci Heap

As you're aware, heaps primarily serve to implement priority queues, and the Fibonacci heap outperforms binomial and binary heaps in terms of time complexity. The amortized time complexities for various operations in a Fibonacci heap are outlined below:

1. Find Min - $\Theta(1)$, equivalent to binomial and binary heaps.
2. Delete Min - $O(Logn)$, which matches $\Theta(Logn)$ in binomial and binary heaps.
3. Insert - $\Theta(1)$, compared to $\Theta(Logn)$ in binary heaps and $\Theta(1)$ in binomial heaps.
4. Decrease-Key - $\Theta(1)$, contrasting with $\Theta(Logn)$ in binomial and binary heaps.
5. Merge - $\Theta(1)$, in contrast to $\Theta(m\ Logn)$ or $\Theta(m+n)$ in binary heaps and $\Theta(Logn)$ in binomial heaps.

Similar to the binomial heap, the Fibonacci heap consists of a series of trees adhering to the max-heap or min-heap property. However, Fibonacci trees can take on any shape, including all being single nodes, unlike the binomial heap where all trees must be binomial.

The Fibonacci heap maintains a pointer to the minimum value (tree root), and a doubly-linked list connects all the trees. This enables a single pointer to access all of them.

The key concept revolves around a "lazy" execution of operations. For instance, the merge operation merely links two heaps, and the insert operation is as straightforward as adding a new tree with a single node. The most intricate operation is extracting the minimum, which involves consolidating trees, making the delete operation somewhat complex as it requires decreasing the key to minimum infinite before calling the extract-minimum operation.

Noteworthy Points:

1. The Decrease-Key operation significantly reduces time complexity, crucial for Prim and Djikstra algorithms. While using a binary heap results in a time complexity of O(VLogV + ELogV), employing a Fibonacci heap improves it to O(VLogV + E).
2. Despite promising time complexity, real-world performance of Fibonacci heaps has been somewhat slow due to high hidden constants.
3. The name "Fibonacci heaps" originates from the usage of Fibonacci numbers in the running time analysis. Additionally, all nodes in a Fibonacci heap have a maximum O(Logn) degree. When a subtree has its root in a node of degree k, its size is a minimum of F k+2, and the kth Fibonacci number is F k.

Insertion and Union

Now, let's delve into two Fibonacci heap operations, beginning with insertion.

Insertion Algorithm:

1. Create a new node, x.
2. Check if heap H is empty.
3. If empty, set x as the single node in the root list, and update the H(min) pointer to x.
4. If not empty, insert x into the root list, and update H(min).

Union

To merge two Fibonacci heaps, H1 and H2, the following algorithm can be employed:

1. Concatenate the root lists of H1 and H2 into a single Fibonacci heap, H.
2. If the minimum value of H1 (H1(min)) is less than the minimum value of H2 (H2(min)), set H(min) to H2(min).
3. Otherwise, set H(min) to H1(min).

The C++ program below demonstrates the creation of a Fibonacci heap and insertion into it:

```
// C++ program to demonstrate building
// and a Fibonacci heap and inserting into it
#include
```

```cpp
#include
#include
using namespace std;

struct node {
    node* parent;
    node* child;
    node* left;
    node* right;
    int key;
};

// Create min pointer as "mini"
    struct node* mini = NULL;

// Declare an integer for the number of nodes in the heap
    int no_of_nodes = 0;

// Function to insert a node in the heap
    void insertion(int val) {
    struct node* new_node = (struct node*)malloc(sizeof(struct node));
    new_node->key = val;
    new_node->parent = NULL;
    new_node->child = NULL;
    new_node->left = new_node;
    new_node->right = new_node;

if (mini != NULL) {
    (mini->left)->right = new_node;
    new_node->right = mini;
```

```
new_node->left = mini->left;
mini->left = new_node;
if (new_node->key < mini->key)
mini = new_node;
} else {
mini = new_node;
}
}

// Function to display the heap
   void display(struct node* mini) {
   node* ptr = mini;
   if (ptr == NULL)
   cout << "The Heap is Empty" << endl;
   else {
   cout << "The root nodes of Heap are: " << endl;
   do {
   cout << ptr->key;
   ptr = ptr->right;
   if (ptr != mini) {
   cout << "—>";
   }
   } while (ptr != mini && ptr->right != NULL);
   cout << endl
   << "The heap has " << no_of_nodes << " nodes" << endl;
   }
}

// Function to find the min node in the heap
   void find_min(struct node* mini) {
   cout << "min of heap is: " << mini->key << endl;
```

```
}

// Driver code
  int main() {
  no_of_nodes = 7;
  insertion(4);
  insertion(3);
  insertion(7);
  insertion(5);
  insertion(2);
  insertion(1);
  insertion(10);

display(mini);
  find_min(mini);
  return 0;
  }
```

Output:
The root nodes of Heap are: 1—>2—>3—>4—>7—>5—>10 The heap has 7 nodes Min of heap is: 1

Fibonacci Heap – Removal, Extract Minimum, and Key Reduction

After exploring insertion and union operations, pivotal for understanding subsequent actions, let's delve into Extract_min().

Extract_min()

This operation involves a function to eradicate the minimum node, adjusting the min pointer to the lowest value in the remaining heap. The algorithm proceeds as follows:

1. Delete the min node.
2. Set the head to the next min node. Subsequently, add all trees from the deleted node to the root list.
3. Create an array with degree pointers matching the size of the deleted node.
4. Set the degree pointer to the current node.
5. Move to the next node. If the degrees are identical, employ the union operation to merge the trees. If they differ, set the degree pointer to the next node.
6. Repeat steps four and five until the heap is processed.

Decrease_key()

To decrease the value of any heap element, follow this algorithm:

1. Decrease node x's value to the specified new value.
2. Case 1: If this maintains the min-heap property, update the min pointer if necessary.

3. Case 2: If this violates the min-heap property and x's parent is unmarked, perform the following:

a. Cut off the link between x and the parent.
b. Mark x's parent.
c. Add the tree rooted at x to the root list, updating the min pointer if required.

4. Case 3: If a violation occurs, and x's parent is already marked:

a. Cut off the link between x and p[x] (the parent).
b. Add x to the root list, updating the min pointer if needed.
c. Cut off the link between p[x] and p[p[x]].
d. Add p[x] to the root list, updating the min pointer if necessary.
e. Mark p[p[x]] if unmarked.
f. Otherwise, cut off p[p[x]], and repeat steps 4b to 4e, using p[p[x]] as x.

Deletion()

Follow this algorithm to delete an element from the heap:

1. Decrease the value of the node (x) to be deleted to a minimum using the Decrease_key() function.
2. Heapify the heap with x, adhering to the min-heap property and placing x in the root list.
3. Apply Extract_min() to the heap.

C++ Program Illustrating Extract_min, Deletion, and Decrease_key Operations

Here's a C++ program showcasing the Extract_min, Deletion, and Decrease_key operations:

```cpp
#include
    #include
    #include
    #include
    using namespace std;

// Define a structure to represent a node in the heap
    struct node {
    node* parent; // Parent pointer
    node* child; // Child pointer
    node* left; // Pointer to the node on the left
    node* right; // Pointer to the node on the right
    int key; // Value of the node
    int degree; // Degree of the node
    char mark; // Black or white mark of the node
    char c; // Flag for assisting in the Find node function
    };

// Create min pointer as "mini"
    struct node* mini = NULL;

// Declare an integer for the number of nodes in the heap
    int no_of_nodes = 0;

// Function to insert a node into the heap
```

```c
void insertion(int val) {
    struct node* new_node = new node();
    new_node->key = val;
    new_node->degree = 0;
    new_node->mark = 'W';
    new_node->c = 'N';
    new_node->parent = NULL;
    new_node->child = NULL;
    new_node->left = new_node;
    new_node->right = new_node;

if (mini != NULL) {
   (mini->left)->right = new_node;
   new_node->right = mini;
   new_node->left = mini->left;
   mini->left = new_node;

if (new_node->key < mini->key)
   mini = new_node;
   } else {
   mini = new_node;
   }

no_of_nodes++;
   }

// Link the heap nodes in the parent-child relationship
    void Fibonnaci_link(struct node* ptr2, struct node* ptr1) {
    (ptr2->left)->right = ptr2->right;
    (ptr2->right)->left = ptr2->left;
```

```c
if (ptr1->right == ptr1)
  mini = ptr1;

ptr2->left = ptr2;
  ptr2->right = ptr2;
  ptr2->parent = ptr1;

if (ptr1->child == NULL)
  ptr1->child = ptr2;

ptr2->right = ptr1->child;
  ptr2->left = (ptr1->child)->left;
  ((ptr1->child)->left)->right = ptr2;
  (ptr1->child)->left = ptr2;

if (ptr2->key < (ptr1->child)->key)
  ptr1->child = ptr2;

ptr1->degree++;
  }

// Consolidate the heap
  void Consolidate() {
  int temp1;
  float temp2 = (log(no_of_nodes)) / (log(2));
  int temp3 = temp2;
  struct node* arr[temp3 + 1];

for (int i = 0; i <= temp3; i++)
  arr[i] = NULL;
```

```
node* ptr1 = mini;
  node* ptr2;
  node* ptr3;
  node* ptr4 = ptr1;

do {
  ptr4 = ptr4->right;
  temp1 = ptr1->degree;

while (arr[temp1] != NULL) {
  ptr2 = arr[temp1];

if (ptr1->key > ptr2->key) {
  ptr3 = ptr1;
  ptr1 = ptr2;
  ptr2 = ptr3;
  }

if (ptr2 == mini)
  mini = ptr1;

Fibonnaci_link(ptr2, ptr1);

if (ptr1->right == ptr1)
  mini = ptr1;

arr[temp1] = NULL;
  temp1++;
  }

arr[temp1] = ptr1;
```

```
    ptr1 = ptr1->right;
  } while (ptr1 != mini);

  mini = NULL;

  for (int j = 0; j <= temp3; j++) {
    if (arr[j] != NULL) {
    arr[j]->left = arr[j];
    arr[j]->right = arr[j];

  if (mini != NULL) {
    (mini->left)->right = arr[j];
    arr[j]->right = mini;
    arr[j]->left = mini->left;
    mini->left = arr[j];

  if (arr[j]->key < mini->key)
    mini = arr[j];
    } else {
    mini = arr[j];
    }

  if (mini == NULL)
    mini = arr[j];
    else if (arr[j]->key < mini->key)
    mini = arr[j];
    }
    }
    }

// Function to extract the minimum node in the heap
```

```cpp
void Extract_min() {
if (mini == NULL)
cout << "The heap is empty" << endl;
else {
node* temp = mini;
node* pntr;
pntr = temp;
node* x = NULL;

if (temp->child != NULL) {
   x = temp->child;

do {
   pntr = x->right;
   (mini->left)->right = x;
   x->right = mini;
   x->left = mini->left;
   mini->left = x;

if (x->key < mini->key)
   mini = x;

x->parent = NULL;
   x = pntr;
   } while (pntr != temp->child);
   }

(temp->left)->right = temp->right;
   (temp->right)->left = temp->left;
   mini = temp->right;
```

```
if (temp == temp->right && temp->child == NULL)
    mini = NULL;
else {
mini = temp->right;
Consolidate();
}

no_of_nodes—;
    }
    }

// Cut a node in the heap to be placed in the root list
    void Cut(struct node* found, struct node* temp) {
    if (found == found->right)
    temp->child = NULL;

(found->left)->right = found->right;
    (found->right)->left = found->left;

if (found == temp->child)
    temp->child = found->right;

temp->degree = temp->degree - 1;
    found->right = found;
    found->left = found;

(mini->left)->right = found;
    found->right = mini;
    found->left = mini->left;
    mini->left = found;
```

```cpp
found->parent = NULL;
  found->mark = 'B';
  }

// Recursive cascade cutting function
  void Cascase_cut(struct node* temp) {
  node* ptr5 = temp->parent;

if (ptr5 != NULL) {
  if (temp->mark == 'W') {
  temp->mark = 'B';
  } else {
  Cut(temp, ptr5);
  Cascase_cut(ptr5);
  }
  }
  }

// Function to decrease the value of a node in the heap
  void Decrease_key(struct node* found, int val) {
  if (mini == NULL)
  cout << "The Heap is Empty" << endl;

if (found == NULL)
  cout << "Node not found in the Heap" << endl;

found->key = val;
  struct node* temp = found->parent;

if (temp != NULL && found->key < temp->key) {
  Cut(found, temp);
```

```
    Cascase_cut(temp);
  }

if (found->key < mini->key)
  mini = found;
  }


// Function to find the given node
  void Find(struct node* mini, int old_val, int val) {
  struct node* found = NULL;
  node* temp5 = mini;
  temp5->c = 'Y';
  node* found_ptr = NULL;

if (temp5->key == old_val) {
  found_ptr = temp5;
  temp5->c = 'N';
  found = found_ptr;
  Decrease_key(found, val);
  }

if (found_ptr == NULL) {
  if (temp5->child != NULL)
  Find(temp5->child, old_val, val);

if ((temp5->right)->c != 'Y')
  Find(temp5->right, old_val, val);
  }

temp5->c = 'N';
  found = found_ptr;
```

```cpp
}

// Delete a node from the heap
    void Deletion(int val) {
    if (mini == NULL)
    cout « "The heap is empty" « endl;
    else {
    // Decrease the value of the node to 0
    Find(mini, val, 0);
    // Call the Extract_min function to
    // delete the minimum value node, which is 0
    Extract_min();
    cout « "Key Deleted" « endl;
    }
    }

// Function to display the heap
    void display() {
    node* ptr = mini;

if (ptr == NULL)
    cout « "The Heap is Empty" « endl;
    else {
    cout « "The root nodes of Heap are: " « endl;

do {
    cout « ptr->key;

ptr = ptr->right;

if (ptr != mini) {
```

```cpp
        cout « "—>";
    }
} while (ptr != mini && ptr->right != NULL);

cout « endl
    « "The heap has " « no_of_nodes « " nodes" « endl
    « endl;
    }
    }

// Driver code
int main() {
    // Create a heap and insert 3 nodes into it
    cout « "Creating the initial heap" « endl;
    insertion(5);
    insertion(2);
    insertion(8);

    // Display the root list of the heap
    display();

    // Extract the minimum value node from the heap
    cout « "Extracting min" « endl;
    Extract_min();
    display();

    // Decrease the value of node '8' to '7'
    cout « "Decrease the value of 8 to 7" « endl;
    Find(mini, 8, 7);
    display();
```

```
// Delete the node '7'
    cout « "Delete the node 7" « endl;
    Deletion(7);
    display();

return 0;
    }
```
Output:

Creating the initial heap
    The root nodes of Heap are:
    2—>5—>8
    The heap has 3 nodes

Extracting min
    The root nodes of Heap are:
    5
    The heap has 2 nodes

Decrease the value of 8 to 7
    The root nodes of Heap are:
    5
    The heap has 2 nodes

Delete the node 7
    Key Deleted
    The root nodes of Heap are:
    5
    The heap has 1 node

Leftist Heap Overview

Leftist heaps, also recognized as leftist trees, function as priority queues and are an implementation of a binary heap variant. In this structure, every node possesses an "s" value, representing the distance to the nearest leaf. Unlike a binary heap that remains a consistently balanced binary tree, a leftist tree can often be notably imbalanced.

The time complexities of leftist heaps are outlined below:

1. Get Min:O(1), aligning with binomial and binary heaps.
2. Delete Min: O(Logn), comparable to binomial and binary heaps.
3. Insert:O(Logn), distinct from the binary heap's O(Logn) and binomial heap's O(1). The worst-case scenario is O(Logn).
4. Merge: O(Logn), akin to the binomial heap.

Leftist trees or heaps adhere to binary tree characteristics:

1. The standard Min Heap property: key(i) >= key(parent(i)).
2. Left side heaviness: dist(right(i)) <= dist(left(i)). Here, dist(i) signifies the number of edges on the shortest path between node i and a leaf node in an extended binary tree. Null children are considered as leaves or external nodes. The shortest path to a descendant external node always traverses the right child. All subtrees are leftist trees, and dist(i) = 1 + dist(right(i)).

Example:

The tree below illustrates each node's distance calculated according to the aforementioned procedure. The rightmost node has a rank of 0 because its right subtree is null, and its parent's distance is 1 (dist(i) = 1 + dist(right(i))). All nodes follow this procedure, calculating their s-values (rank).

From the second property above, two conclusions can be drawn:

1. The shortest path from the root to a leaf is the path to the rightmost leaf.
2. If x nodes exist on the path to the rightmost leaf, the leftist heap has a minimum of 2x − 1 nodes. This implies a path length of O(Logn) where the leftist heap has n nodes.

Operations:

1. merge(): The primary operation.
2. deleteMin() or extractMin(): Removes the root and calls merge() for the right and left subtrees.
3. insert(): Creates leftist trees with single keys. Calls merge() for the specified tree and the tree with a single node.

Now, let's delve into the merge() operation in more detail.
This operation merges the right subtree from one tree with another. Abstract steps include:

1. Setting the root with the smallest value as the new root.
2. Hanging the left subtree on the left.
3. Recursively merging the right subtree with the other tree.
4. Before returning from recursion:

- Updating dist() in the merged root.
   - Swapping left and right subtrees below the root if necessary to maintain the leftist property.

Detailed steps:

1. Compare the roots of both heaps.
2. Push the smaller key into an empty stack, then move to the smaller key's right child.
3. Recursively compare the two keys, pushing the smaller key and moving to the key's right child.
4. Repeat these steps until reaching a null node.
5. Make the last processed node the right child for the top-most node in the stack. If the leftist heap properties are violated, convert the right child into a leftist heap.
6. Continue to recursively pop elements from the stack, converting them into the right child of the new top-most stack node.

Example:

When merging leftist heaps, if the leftist heap property is violated by a subtree (e.g., node 7), it is swapped with the left child to retain the leftist heap property. Subsequently, it is converted into a leftist heap, and the process repeats.

The worst-case time complexity of this algorithm is O(Logn), where n denotes the number of nodes in the leftist heap.

C++ Implementation of Leftist Heap

Here is a C++ implementation of a leftist heap:

```
#include
using namespace std;

// Node Class Declaration
    class LeftistNode {
    public:
    int element;
    LeftistNode *left;
    LeftistNode *right;
    int dist;

LeftistNode(int &element, LeftistNode *lt = NULL,
    LeftistNode *rt = NULL, int np = 0) {
    this->element = element;
    right = rt;
    left = lt;
```

```
    dist = np;
  }
};
```

// Class Declaration
```
  class LeftistHeap {
  public:
  LeftistHeap();
  LeftistHeap(LeftistHeap &rhs);
  ~LeftistHeap();
  bool isEmpty();
  bool isFull();
  int &findMin();
  void Insert(int &x);
  void deleteMin();
  void deleteMin(int &minItem);
  void makeEmpty();
  void Merge(LeftistHeap &rhs);
  LeftistHeap &operator=(LeftistHeap &rhs);

  private:
    LeftistNode *root;
    LeftistNode *Merge(LeftistNode *h1, LeftistNode *h2);
    LeftistNode *Merge1(LeftistNode *h1, LeftistNode *h2);
    void swapChildren(LeftistNode *t);
    void reclaimMemory(LeftistNode *t);
    LeftistNode *clone(LeftistNode *t);
  };
```

// Construct the leftist heap
```
  LeftistHeap::LeftistHeap() {
```

```
    root = NULL;
}

// Copy constructor.
    LeftistHeap::LeftistHeap(LeftistHeap &rhs) {
    root = NULL;
    *this = rhs;
}

// Destruct the leftist heap
    LeftistHeap::~LeftistHeap() {
    makeEmpty();
}

/* Merge RHS into the priority queue.
    RHS becomes empty. RHS must be different
    from this.*/
    void LeftistHeap::Merge(LeftistHeap &rhs) {
    if (this == &rhs)
    return;
    root = Merge(root, rhs.root);
    rhs.root = NULL;
}

/* Internal method to merge two roots.
    Deals with deviant cases and calls recursive Merge1.*/
    LeftistNode *LeftistHeap::Merge(LeftistNode *h1, LeftistNode *h2) {
    if (h1 == NULL)
    return h2;
    if (h2 == NULL
```

```
    return h1;
    if (h1->element < h2->element)
    return Merge1(h1, h2);
    else
    return Merge1(h2, h1);
}
```

```
/* Internal method to merge two roots.
   Assumes trees are not empty, and h1's root contains
   the smallest item.*/
   LeftistNode *LeftistHeap::Merge1(LeftistNode *h1, LeftistNode *h2) {
     if (h1->left == NULL)
     h1->left = h2;
     else {
     h1->right = Merge(h1->right, h2);
     if (h1->left->dist < h1->right->dist)
     swapChildren(h1);
     h1->dist = h1->right->dist + 1;
     }
     return h1;
   }
```

```
// Swaps t's two children.
   void LeftistHeap::swapChildren(LeftistNode *t) {
     LeftistNode *tmp = t->left;
     t->left = t->right;
     t->right = tmp;
   }
```

/* Insert item x into the priority queue, maintaining

heap order.*/
void LeftistHeap::Insert(int &x) {
root = Merge(new LeftistNode(x), root);
}

/* Find the smallest item in the priority queue.
Return the smallest item, or throw Underflow if empty.*/
int &LeftistHeap::findMin() {
return root->element;
}

/* Remove the smallest item from the priority queue.
Throws Underflow if empty.*/
void LeftistHeap::deleteMin() {
LeftistNode *oldRoot = root;
root = Merge(root->left, root->right);
delete oldRoot;
}

/* Remove the smallest item from the priority queue.
Pass the smallest item back, or throw Underflow if empty.*/
void LeftistHeap::deleteMin(int &minItem) {
if (isEmpty()) {
cout « "Heap is Empty" « endl;
return;
}
minItem = findMin();
deleteMin();
}

/* Test if the priority queue is logically empty.

```cpp
 Returns true if empty, false otherwise*/
bool LeftistHeap::isEmpty() {
return root == NULL;
}


/* Test if the priority queue is logically full.
   Returns false in this implementation.*/
   bool LeftistHeap::isFull() {
   return false;
   }


// Make the priority queue logically empty
   void LeftistHeap::makeEmpty() {
   reclaimMemory(root);
   root = NULL;
   }


// Deep copy
   LeftistHeap &LeftistHeap::operator=(LeftistHeap &rhs) {
   if (this != &rhs) {
   makeEmpty();
   root = clone(rhs.root);
   }
   return *this;
   }


// Internal method to make the tree empty.
   void LeftistHeap::reclaimMemory(LeftistNode *t) {
   if (t != NULL) {
   reclaimMemory(t->left);
   reclaimMemory(t->right);
```

```
        delete t;
    }
}

// Internal method to clone the subtree.
    LeftistNode *LeftistHeap::clone(LeftistNode *t) {
    if (t == NULL)
    return NULL;
    else
    return new LeftistNode(t->element, clone(t->left),
    clone(t->right), t->dist);
    }

// Driver program
    int main() {
    LeftistHeap h;
    LeftistHeap h1;
    LeftistHeap h2;
    int x;
    int arr[] = {1, 5, 7, 10, 15};
    int arr1[] = {22, 75};

h.Insert(arr[0]);
    h.Insert(arr[1]);
    h.Insert(arr[2]);
    h.Insert(arr[3]);
    h.Insert(arr[4]);
    h1.Insert(arr1[0]);
    h1.Insert(arr1[1]);

h.deleteMin(x);
```

```
    cout << x << endl;

h1.deleteMin(x);
    cout << x << endl;

h.Merge(h1);
    h2 = h;
    h2.deleteMin(x);
    cout << x << endl;

return 0;
}
```
Output:
1
22
5

K-ary Heap

The K-ary heap, an extension of the binary heap where each node has k children instead of 2 (when k equals 2), shares fundamental properties with the binary heap:

1. A K-ary heap forms an almost complete binary tree, with all levels, except the last, being fully occupied from left to right.

2. Similar to the binary heap, K-ary heaps can be categorized as:
    a. Max K-ary heap – the root key surpasses all descendants,

recursively true for each node.

b. Min K-ary heap – the root key is smaller than the descendants, recursively true for each node.

Examples:

In a 3-ary max heap:
```
10
/ | \
7 9 8
/|\
4 6 5 7
```

In a 3-ary min heap:
```
10
/ | \
12 11 13
/|\
14 15 18
```

A complete K-ary tree with n nodes has a height given by logkn.

Applications of K-Ary Heap:

1. In a priority queue implementation, K-ary heaps have a faster decrease_key() operation compared to binary heaps. While the binary heap's time complexity is O(Log2n), the K-ary heap is O(Logkn). However, this efficiency comes at the cost of an increased time complexity for the extractMin() operation, O(k log ln) for K-ary heaps compared to O(Log2n) for binary heaps. This makes K-ary heaps suitable for algorithms where decrease priority operations are more common than extractMin(), such as Prim and Dijkstra algorithms.

2. K-ary heaps exhibit better memory cache behavior than binary heaps, resulting in practical speed improvements. However, their worst-case running times for delete() and extractMin() operations are larger, both being O(K Log kn).

Implementation:

Represented using an array with 0-based indexing, a K-ary heap follows these rules for any node at index i:
   - For the node at index i (excluding the root node), the parent is at index (i-1)/k.
   - Children of the node at index i are located at indices (k*i)+1, (k*i)+2, ..., (k*i)+k.
   - In a heap of size n, the last non-leaf node is at (n-2)/k.

buildHeap():

This function takes an input array and builds a heap. Starting from the last non-leaf node, the loop runs to the root, and for each index, restoreDown (or maxHeapify) is called to ensure the node is in its correct place, moving down the heap and building it from the bottom up.

The loop starts from the last non-leaf node because nodes after that are leaf nodes, trivially satisfying the heap property.

restoreDown() (or maxHeapify):

This function maintains the heap property by iterating through the node's children, finding the maximum, and swapping if necessary. This process continues until the node is back in its original position within the K-ary heap.

extractMax():

This function extracts the root node, returning it after copying the last node to the root. RestoreDown is then called on the root to maintain the heap property.

insert():

Inserts a node at the last position, and restoreUp() is called on the index to put the node in its rightful position. RestoreUp compares the node iteratively with its parent, swapping them when the node's key is greater than the parent's key.

C++ Implementation of K-ary Heap Operations

In the subsequent C++ code, we consolidate all the operations of a k-ary heap:

```
// C++ program to demonstrate all the operations of
// k-ary Heap
#include
using namespace std;

// Function to heapify (or restore the max-heap
    // property). This is used to build a k-ary heap
    // and in extractMin()
    // att[] — Array that stores heap
    // len — Size of array
    // index — index of element to be restored
    // (or heapified)
    void restoreDown(int arr[], int len, int index, int k) {
    // child array to store indexes of all
    // the children of the given node
    int child[k+1];
    while (1) {
    // child[i]=-1 if the node is a leaf
```

```
// children (no children)
for (int i=1; i<=k; i++)
child[i] = ((k*index + i) < len) ? (k*index + i) : -1;
// max_child stores the maximum child, and
// max_child_index holds its index
int max_child = -1, max_child_index;
// loop to find the maximum of all
// the children of a given node
for (int i=1; i<=k; i++) {
if (child[i] != -1 && arr[child[i]] > max_child) {
max_child_index = child[i];
max_child = arr[child[i]];
}
}
// leaf node
if (max_child == -1)
break;
// only swap if the max_child_index key
// is greater than the node's key
if (arr[index] < arr[max_child_index])
swap(arr[index], arr[max_child_index]);
index = max_child_index;
}
}

// Restores a given node up in the heap. This is used
    // in decreaseKey() and insert()
    void restoreUp(int arr[], int index, int k) {
    // parent stores the index of the parent variable
    // of the node
    int parent = (index-1)/k;
```

```
// Loop should run only until the root node in case the
// element inserted is the maximum. restoreUp will
// send it to the root node
while (parent >= 0) {
if (arr[index] > arr[parent]) {
swap(arr[index], arr[parent]);
index = parent;
parent = (index -1)/k;
}
// the node has been restored in the correct position
else
break;
}
}


// Function to build a heap of arr[0..n-1] and value of k.
   void buildHeap(int arr[], int n, int k) {
   // all internal nodes are heapified starting from the last
   // non-leaf node up to the root node
   // and calling restoreDown on each
   for (int i = (n-1)/k; i >= 0; i—)
   restoreDown(arr, n, i, k);
}


// Function to insert a value in a heap. The parameters are
   // the array, size of the heap, value k, and the element to
   // be inserted
   void insert(int arr[], int* n, int k, int elem) {
   // Put the new element in the last position
   arr[*n] = elem;
   // Increase heap size by 1
```

```c
    *n = *n + 1;
    // Call restoreUp on the last index
    restoreUp(arr, *n-1, k);
}

// Function to return the key of the heap's root node
    // and restore the heap property for the remaining nodes
    int extractMax(int arr[], int* n, int k) {
    // Stores the key of root node to be returned
    int max = arr[0];
    // Copy the last node's key to the root node
    arr[0] = arr[*n-1];
    // Decrease heap size by 1
    *n = *n - 1;
    // Call restoreDown on the root node to restore
    // it to the correct position in the heap
    restoreDown(arr, *n, 0, k);
    return max;
}

// Driver program
    int main() {
    const int capacity = 100;
    int arr[capacity] = {4, 5, 6, 7, 8, 9, 10};
    int n = 7;
    int k = 3;
    buildHeap(arr, n, k);
    printf("Built Heap : \n");
    for (int i = 0; i < n; i++)
    printf("%d ", arr[i]);
    int element = 3;
```

```
insert(arr, &n, k, element);
printf("\n\nHeap after insertion of %d: \n", element);
for (int i = 0; i < n; i++)
printf("%d ", arr[i]);
printf("\n\nExtracted max is %d", extractMax(arr, &n, k));
printf("\n\nHeap after extract max: \n");
for (int i = 0; i < n; i++)
printf("%d ", arr[i]);
return 0;
}
```

Output:
Built Heap :
10 9 6 7 8 4 5
Heap after insertion of 3:
10 9 6 7 8 4 5 3
Extracted max is 10
Heap after extract max:
9 8 6 7 3 4 5

Time Complexity of K-ary Heap Operations

In a k-ary heap with n nodes, the maximum height of the heap is logkn. The restoreUp() function iterates no more than logkn times, as it moves the node up a level in each iteration or down a level when restoreDown() is utilized.

The time complexity of restoreDown() is O(klogkn) since it recursively calls itself for k children. For both decreaseKey() and insert() operations, restoreUp is invoked only once, resulting in a time complexity of O(klogkn).

The extractMax() function calls restoreDown() once, giving

it a time complexity of O(klogkn). The build heap operation has a time complexity of O(n), comparable to that of a binary heap.

Heapsort and Iterative HeapSort

Before delving into the iterative heapsort data structure, it's essential to grasp the fundamentals of heapsort. This sorting technique relies on comparisons and is grounded in the binary heap structure. Similar to selection sort, it locates the minimum element, places it at the top, and repeats the process for the remaining elements.

Binary heaps, complete binary trees storing items in specific orders (e.g., max heap or min-heap), can be represented by arrays. If a parent node is at index I, the left child is at 2 * I, and the right child is at 2 * I + 2.

Heapsort Algorithm:

1. Utilize the input data to construct a max heap.
2. Store the largest item in the heap's root, replace it with the last item, and decrease the heap size by 1. Heapify the tree's root.
3. Repeat the previous step until the heap size reaches or falls below 1.

Building the Heap: Heapification can only be applied from the bottom up to a node whose children have already been heapified. In this process, the heap is constructed top-down, with the heapify procedure recursively calling itself.

Example: Input data: 4, 10, 3, 5, 1

4(0)
/ \
10(1) 3(2)
/ \
5(3) 1(4)
Apply heapify to index 1:
4(0)
/ \
10(1) 3(2)
/ \
5(3) 1(4)
Apply heapify to index 0:
10(0)
/ \
5(1) 3(2)
/ \
4(3) 1(4)

The heap is built top-down with the heapify process, recursively calling itself.

Heapsort Implementation in C++:

```
// C++ program to perform Heapsort
  #include
  using namespace std;


// Function to heapify a subtree rooted at node i, where i is an index in arr[] and n is the heap size
  void heapify(int arr[], int n, int i) {
  int largest = i; // Initialize the largest element as the root
  int l = 2 * i + 1; // left child = 2*i + 1
```

```
    int r = 2 * i + 2; // right child = 2*i + 2

// If the left child is larger than the root
    if (l < n && arr[l] > arr[largest])
    largest = l;

// If the right child is larger than the largest so far
    if (r < n && arr[r] > arr[largest])
    largest = r;

// If the largest is not the root
    if (largest != i) {
    swap(arr[i], arr[largest]);
    // Recursively heapify the affected sub-tree
    heapify(arr, n, largest);
    }
    }

// Main function to perform heapsort
    void heapSort(int arr[], int n) {
    // Build the heap (rearrange the array)
    for (int i = n / 2 - 1; i >= 0; i—)
    heapify(arr, n, i);

// Extract elements from the heap one by one
    for (int i = n - 1; i > 0; i—) {
    // Move the current root to the end
    swap(arr[0], arr[i]);
    // Call heapify on the reduced heap
    heapify(arr, i, 0);
    }
```

```
}
```

```
// Utility function to print an array of size n
    void printArray(int arr[], int n) {
    for (int i = 0; i < n; ++i)
    cout « arr[i] « " ";
    cout « "\n";
    }
```

```
// Driver code
    int main() {
    int arr[] = {12, 11, 13, 5, 6, 7};
    int n = sizeof(arr) / sizeof(arr[0]);
```

```
// Call heapsort on the array
    heapSort(arr, n);
```

```
// Display the sorted array
    cout « "Sorted array is \n";
    printArray(arr, n);
```

```
return 0;
    }
```

Output:

Sorted array is
    5 6 7 11 12 13

Time Complexity:

The heapify operation has a time complexity of O(Logn), the createAndBuildHeap() function has a time complexity of O(n), and the overall time complexity of heapsort is O(nLogn).

Advantages of Heapsort Algorithm

Efficiency:

Heapsort exhibits logarithmic time complexity, ensuring efficiency as the sorting list size increases. This is in contrast to many other algorithms, which experience exponential slowdowns with larger datasets.

Memory Usage:

The algorithm is highly memory-efficient, requiring minimal additional space beyond the initial sorting list.

Simplicity:

Heapsort stands out for its simplicity, making it easy to comprehend. It avoids the use of advanced computer science concepts like recursion, contributing to its straightforward nature.

Detailed Example of Heapsort Algorithm

Consider a more comprehensive illustration of the heapsort algorithm. Initially, a max heap is constructed, and the root element is swapped with the last element while maintaining the heap property to ensure a sorted list.

Example: Input: 10 20 15 17 9 21 Output: 9 10 15 17 20 21

In the max heap construction, elements are compared and swapped as needed. For instance, comparing 20 and 10 leads to the following swaps: 20 10 15 17 9 21 20 17 15 10 9 21 21 17 20 10 9 15

Subsequently, sorting is applied. The first and last elements are swapped, and the max heap property is maintained through multiple iterations until the list is sorted.

C++ Implementation:

```cpp
#include
using namespace std;

void buildMaxHeap(int arr[], int n) {
    // Implementation details for building Max Heap
}

void heapSort(int arr[], int n) {
    // Implementation details for heapsort
}

int main() {
    // Example array and function calls
    int arr[] = {10, 20, 15, 17, 9, 21};
    int n = sizeof(arr) / sizeof(arr[0]);

    printf("Given array: ");
    for (int i = 0; i < n; i++)
        printf("%d ", arr[i]);
    printf("\n\n");
```

heapSort(arr, n);

printf("Sorted array: ");
   for (int i = 0; i < n; i++)
   printf("%d ", arr[i]);

return 0;
}

Output:

Given array: 10 20 15 17 9 21 Sorted array: 9 10 15 17 20 21

Time Complexity:

Both the heapSort and buildMaxHeap functions operate in O(nLogn) time, resulting in an overall time complexity of O(nLogn).

6

Conclusion

Are you questioning the relevance of delving into intricate data structures? Why do job interviews in data science or data engineering emphasize questions about them? Many individuals, both novice and seasoned programmers, often sidestep learning about algorithms and data structures, citing their complexity and apparent lack of practicality.

Nevertheless, acquiring knowledge of data structures and algorithms provides a lens through which real-world problems and their solutions can be viewed in code. It equips you with the skills to dissect a problem into smaller components, contemplate their interconnections, and devise an efficient final solution by strategically incorporating enhancements along the way.

This guide has navigated you through advanced data structures integral to algorithms, offering insights into their functionalities and optimal applications. Recognizing its advanced nature, it acknowledges that immediate comprehensive understanding is not anticipated. Instead, consider utilizing this guide as a reference when evaluating whether a particular data structure suits your situation or exploring alternative, more effective approaches.

Appreciate your time invested in reading this guide. I trust it has proven beneficial, empowering you to progress further in your data journey.

www.ingramcontent.com/pod-product-compliance
Lightning Source LLC
LaVergne TN
LVHW011942070526
838202LV00054B/4752